THE SUMMA ILLUMINATED

"This book is the ordinary reader's clearest introduction to the *Summa Theologica*. It illuminates the obscure and enlivens the dispassionate arguments of St. Thomas Aquinas. You'll not only get Thomas's point; you'll know why it's important. The *Summa* is a book that can change your mind and your life for the better. *The Summa Illuminated* is the book that will make your reading possible and enjoyable. Everyone should be reading St. Thomas, and I can't imagine a better guide to his work than Fr. Cajetan Cuddy."

Scott Hahn
Catholic author and theologian

"*The Summa Illuminated* offers a clear, straightforward road map to first-time readers of Aquinas's most famous and enduringly influential work. Fr. Cuddy's short summaries of the main themes in each group of questions are helpful in orienting the reader to the basics of Aquinas's system. This is certainly a book you want by your side as you begin to explore the wonderful world of the *Summa Theologica*."

Thérèse Scarpelli Cory
Associate professor of Thomistic studies at the University of Notre Dame

"*The Summa Illuminated* gives invaluable assistance to those who want to know the thought of St. Thomas but are stymied by unfamiliar vocabulary and procedure. Fr. Cuddy has provided a way for the 'educated nonexpert' to acquire the treasures of the *Summa*."

Laura Berquist
Founder of Mother of Divine Grace School

"Fr. Cajetan Cuddy's *The Summa Illuminated* offers a penetrating and accessible overview of Aquinas's *Summa*, presenting its overarching structure and key questions with clarity. The final section on the sacraments is especially rich, inviting deeper reflection and union with Jesus Christ."

Austin Habash
Host of the *Summa in a Year* podcast

"In my study of St. Thomas Aquinas, I have learned such a great deal from Fr. Cajetan Cuddy. His sober appreciation for the most pertinent principles and his great facility in theological discourse make him an excellent teacher and guide. *The Summa Illuminated* will certainly prove of great service to all with an appetite for wisdom."

Fr. Gregory Pine, OP
Assistant director of the Thomistic Institute

"To the newcomer, the *Summa Theologica* can be daunting, mysterious, puzzling. In *The Summa Illuminated*, Fr. Cuddy aims to make Aquinas's theological masterpiece more readily accessible. Fr. Cuddy succeeds in his task. Writing in a straightforward, unaffected style, he lays bare the *Summa*'s structure and purpose and the driving concerns of its main parts. *The Summa Illuminated* is a reliable guide, one that will go a long way to making engagement with arguably the greatest presentation and investigation of the Catholic faith even more fruitful and rewarding."

Joseph Wawrykow
Professor emeritus of theology at the University of Notre Dame and author of *The Westminster Handbook to Thomas Aquinas*

The Summa Illuminated

A GUIDE TO
ST. THOMAS AQUINAS'S
MASTERPIECE

CAJETAN CUDDY, OP

Scripture texts and *Summa Theologica* texts are taken from *Summa Theologica* by St. Thomas Aquinas, translated by Fathers of the English Dominican Province, © 1948 by Benzinger Bros., New York, NY.

Nihil Obstat: Reverend Monsignor Michael Heintz, PhD
Censor Librorum

Imprimatur: Most Reverend Kevin C. Rhoades
Bishop of Fort Wayne–South Bend
Given at Fort Wayne, Indiana, on September 22, 2025

The *Nihil Obstat* and *Imprimatur* are official declarations that a book or pamphlet is free of doctrinal or moral error. No implication is contained therein that those who have granted the *Nihil Obstat* or *Imprimatur* agree with its contents, opinions, or statements expressed.

Founded in 1865, Ave Maria Press is a ministry of the United States Province of Holy Cross.

www.avemariapress.com

Paperback: ISBN-13 978-1-64680-393-4

E-book: ISBN-13 978-1-64680-394-1

Cover and text design by Christopher D. Tobin.

Printed and bound in the United States of America.

Library of Congress Cataloging-in-Publication Data is available.

To Professor George Van Pelt ("Van") Campbell,
my first mentor in theology.
The friend who loaned me his copy of
St. Thomas Aquinas's masterpiece.

Contents

Introduction

I first picked up the *Summa Theologica* (*ST*) as a teenager. I was curious about Christian theology, and a friend mentioned to me that St. Thomas Aquinas was one of history's most learned and influential theologians. Filled with anticipation, I picked up the first volume of St. Thomas's summary of the Christian religion and began reading on page one.

A few short paragraphs later, I found myself perplexed and frustrated. Some of the terms that I read were familiar to me—I had a general understanding of what "philosophy," "science," and "sacred doctrine" meant, for example. Other words, however, confused me deeply. I can still vividly remember the puzzlement I suffered regarding Aquinas's use of the word "accident." In my vocabulary, "accident" referred to an unintended event. In Aquinas's lexicon, however, "accident" seemed to refer to something specific and elusive (quite different than "accidentally" dropping a glass vase).

My initial exposure to the *ST* took place in the days before the internet. So I turned to other books for help in my quest to discover what Aquinas was talking about. My search for illuminating books, however, was ultimately unsuccessful. The dictionaries I found on my family's modest bookshelf did not provide insight into his technical language. Moreover, books about St. Thomas Aquinas devoted most of their time to the events in his life and to specific elements of his thought. These books were interesting, to be sure, but did not provide what I earnestly sought: clarity about how the *ST*, as a unified work, reflected Aquinas's personal and intellectual commitments.

This is what I intend to provide in the book that you hold in your hands. I have written this introduction to the *Summa Theologica* to serve as the kind of resource that I instinctively sought (but did not find) when I first picked up Aquinas's masterpiece. Consequently, this book will not devote much space to Aquinas's life.[1] Nor will this book serve as an exhaustive overview of Aquinas's thought. Rather, this book is meant to be a guidebook for those who wish to study Aquinas's own book, the *ST*. It is my hope that those who aspire to study Christian doctrine under Aquinas's tutelage will find in this book helpful guidance about how best to approach the *ST*.

The audience for whom I write are educated nonexperts. By educated, I mean readers who enjoy books and ideas. Most of my readers, I assume, have had some level of college education. Advanced education, however, is not required to benefit from this introductory text. The only thing required for benefiting from this book is a sincere and committed desire to enter into the vast intricacy of the *ST*.

This book is aimed at nonexperts. In other words, I do not presuppose any previous expertise in Aquinas's thought or writings. In the pages that follow, I will explain how to navigate through the (initially, quite foreign) ways that Aquinas presents his arguments and analysis. Moreover, I will provide explanations about key terms that Aquinas presupposes his readers would already know intimately. Thus, it is my sincere desire that, by the end of this book, you will possess adequate familiarity with the structure, content, and themes of the *ST* such that you will be able to approach Aquinas's masterpiece without overwhelming intimidation or insuperable frustration.

I feel compelled to clarify, at this point, what this book will *not* do. This book is not intended to serve either as a comprehensive summary of the *ST* or a replacement for reading the *ST* itself. Scholars and saints have been studying the *ST* for about 750 years. The profundity, clarity, and illumination that the *ST* provides is exemplary in the history of Christian theology. Any reader who wishes to know the *ST* must devote themselves to reading the *ST* itself. Thus, this book in no way aspires to replace or exhaust the content of the *ST*. Rather, think of this book as a guided tour of the *ST*—a tour that is meant to facilitate the reader's own study of the work itself.

The *Summa Theologica:* A Literary Cathedral

Some scholars have suggested that had Aquinas not been a philosopher and a theologian, he would have been an *architect*. The reason for this insightful proposal lies in the structural intricacy of his writings—and of his *ST* supremely. Reading the *ST* is, thus, analogous to entering into a vast medieval cathedral. The venerated cathedrals that still stand in European cities are easy to spot. They are unlike any other buildings that tourists encounter. First, they are usually larger than other city buildings. They stand out, enabling cathedrals to attract the eyes of observers from afar. Second, medieval cathedrals are among the most detailed and intricate of all buildings. There is nothing random about the design or layout of medieval cathedrals: Each detail has a purpose and a meaning. This is why it is not uncommon to observe tourists devoting a great deal of time to each part of a cathedral—perhaps even craning their necks looking up at the elegant stained-glass windows and statues that punctuate the building. Cathedrals overwhelm. They compel visitors to slow their pace and lower their volume when entering into their confines. Cathedrals draw the attention of visitors away from themselves to a grandeur that exceeds them.

Cathedrals are, uniquely, simple and complex structures. They are simple insofar as they have one resounding message: God is real. They are complex insofar as they comprise a multitude of parts, pieces, and sections that contribute to the communication of this simple yet profound message. These sacred buildings direct the attention of pilgrims upward and outward.

Aquinas's *ST* is like a literary cathedral. Everything about the *ST* has meaning and purpose. Nothing about this work is random or capricious. It is a text that can hold the attention of readers in one of its individual parts, questions, or articles. But the holistic cohesion of this work can also enrapture readers. Thus, as a single work and in each of its numerous discrete parts, the *ST* invites readers to discover the truth about reality—and, supremely, the truth about God.

The *ST* is, paradoxically, one of the simplest and the most complex books that readers will ever encounter. It is simple because God is supremely one—there is only one God, and he, alone, is the ultimate fulfillment of the human person. This is the end to which the *ST* consistently points. The *ST* is complex because human persons require distinctions, parts, and discrete propositions in order to understand profound truths. The elegance of the *ST*, accordingly, resides in its uncanny ability to accommodate both the complexity of the step-by-step requirements of human learning and the sublimity of the God who eternally is, who created all of reality, and who redeemed a fallen humanity.

In sum, the *ST* is designed to be something akin to a window. Ultimately, Aquinas did not intend for his book to be the ultimate destination of his reader's attention. Aquinas did not desire that either he or the *ST* would be the ultimate object of our fascination. Rather, Aquinas intended that his writings would facilitate his student's appreciation—and adoration—of God. In this respect, Aquinas's *ST* is like a telescope—something through which readers can look to see what Aquinas himself saw and wanted to see with ever-greater clarity: God.

I will attempt to integrate both of these hallmarks—complexity and simplicity—as we proceed through Aquinas's literary cathedral, the *ST*. Consequently, I will occasionally draw attention to specific details and nuances present in Aquinas's text. I will also emphasize the fundamental integrity of the *ST*. As this book is an introduction, I believe it will be of most use to readers if it highlights the forest more than the trees—and the trees primarily in reference to the forest. My emphasis here will be on the "big picture" cohesion of the *ST* so that you possess some familiarity with its essential layout when venturing into its corridors yourself.

Why Read the *Summa Theologica*?

Before we begin our overview of the *ST*, it is perhaps worth pausing briefly to ask: *Why read the* ST *at all?* What makes this work so special? Are there not other theological writings by holy and learned scholars that merit attention and esteem?

The answer to this latter question is, of course, yes! Aquinas is not the only brilliant Christian author. Indeed, the Catholic Church has, to date, designated as "Doctors of the Church" almost forty saintly authors. Aquinas is one of numerous officially revered teachers that Christians can look to for wisdom and insight.

And yet Aquinas is unique—and the Catholic Church has consistently recognized him as such. The reason for his uniqueness was succinctly expressed by one of Aquinas's greatest expositors: the sixteenth-century Italian cardinal, Thomas de Vio Cajetan. In Leo XIII's papal encyclical *Aeterni Patris* (*On the Restoration of Christian Philosophy*), the pope makes Cardinal Cajetan's estimation of Aquinas his own:

> Among the Scholastic Doctors, the chief and master of all towers Thomas Aquinas, who, as Cajetan observes, because "he most venerated the ancient doctors of the Church, in a certain way seems to have inherited the intellect of all." The doctrines of those illustrious men, like the scattered members of a body, Thomas collected together and cemented, distributed in wonderful order, and so increased with important

> additions that he is rightly and deservedly esteemed the special bulwark and glory of the Catholic faith.[2]

Aquinas is "rightly and deservedly esteemed the special bulwark and glory of the Catholic faith" because he "inherited the intellect of all" of the ancient doctors of the Church. Aquinas was not an isolated thinker. He drank deeply from the patrimony of Christian doctrine. The wisdom and insights he absorbed from his theological predecessors enabled him to offer a coherent summary of the whole of the Christian religion.

Consequently, Pope Leo XIII underscores the profound service Aquinas provided for Catholic doctrine. In the *ST*, Aquinas affords readers a comprehensive, fundamental synthesis of virtually all of Christian teaching. This service was not done prior to Aquinas's *ST*. And no single theologian subsequent to Aquinas has produced a work that excels his in scale or in quality. This claim is difficult to contest even today. Even a quick perusal of the *Catechism of the Catholic Church*, for example, reveals the magisterial esteem that Aquinas's *ST* continues to enjoy. The Catholic Church continues to recognize the truth of the Christian faith in Aquinas's expositions of sacred doctrine.

Numerous theologians and doctors have written many other beautiful, profound, and insightful works about the Christian religion. But no other single author or doctor has written a summary of Christian doctrine that matches the comprehensiveness and fidelity of Aquinas's *ST*. As a comprehensive "summary" of the essential elements of Christian theology, the *ST* remains the standard.

Obviously, there are other theological texts that provide clarity and insight into Christian doctrine—and, perhaps, some that provide even more insight than the *ST* about particular aspects of Christian doctrine. The reason that the *ST* stands paramount among all of these other books, however, is simple: Aquinas's *ST* is unparalleled in terms of its simple comprehensiveness. This is a work that generously rewards all those who spend serious time with it. Moreover, it is a work written for the majority of Christian faithful: beginners. Aquinas explicitly designed the *ST* to be of use for theological novices, those who are not—yet—proficient in matters of sacred doctrine.

And it is to Aquinas's solicitude for us, theological beginners, that we now turn in our first chapter.

Preliminary Considerations

Chapter 1

The Prologue to the *Summa Theologica*

Thomas Aquinas once observed that "a small mistake in the beginning is a big one in the end."[1] The importance of beginnings is not difficult to recognize. If we begin a journey facing the wrong direction, we cannot hope to arrive at the desired destination. Small imprecisions at the commencement of an expedition or a task can result in large divergences at the end. This is evident if we consider the example of an archer: Even if an archer's aim is only ill-calculated by a few degrees, the arrow shot will miss the desired target—perhaps entirely.

This is why introductions are so important. Aquinas's prologue to the *Summa Theologica* (*ST*) ensures that his work is perfectly aimed at his desired goal. If there is one word that captures the sense of the *ST*, it is the word "precision," and this prologue reflects Aquinas's profound pedagogical and literary craftmanship.

In these introductory words, we see Aquinas coordinate his essential themes around his desired destination with radical precision. All too frequently, the importance of this prologue is underappreciated. Many readers even skim or skip over it. Although a short text, it merits our close attention as it is here that Aquinas specifies the purpose and orientation of the entire work:

> Because the Teacher of Catholic truth ought not only to teach the proficient, but also to instruct beginners, according to the Apostle: *As unto little ones in Christ, I gave you milk to drink, not meat* (1 Cor 3:1–2), we purpose in this book to treat of whatever belongs to the Christian religion in such a way as may befit the instruction of beginners. (*ST*, Prologue)

Aquinas orients the *ST* around three coordinating principles: (1) the "Teacher of Catholic truth," (2) the "instruction of beginners," and (3) the "Christian religion." Each of these three principles is essential to understanding what follows in the *ST*. Thus, let us consider them singly as well as collectively.

The Teacher of Catholic Truth

Aquinas utilizes the word "teacher" (in Latin, *doctor*) in a very precise sense. Today, teaching is a very broad category of activity that comprises many different types of persons and many different kinds of instruction. In the thirteenth century, however, teaching Catholic truth was not a mere job. Nor was it only a profession. Rather, teaching Catholic truth reflected the entirety of the teacher's life, calling, and office. Aquinas did not write the *ST* in order to augment his *curriculum vitae* or to obtain tenure at a university. He composed the *ST* in fulfillment of his sacred and public vocation as a Catholic priest and Dominican friar: to teach the truth.

"Teacher of Catholic truth" was not a title that someone could assume unilaterally. It was a holy office—one that was given to highly learned and rigorously trained clerics—officially imparted by the Catholic Church. The office of teacher was nothing short of a sacred vocation. In the thirteenth century, the study of theology was inextricably linked to priestly ministry. Thus, all teachers and students of theology were consecrated to the truth about God. And this truth was not something ethereal or merely professional. Theology was a discipline ordered to the celebration of the sacraments, to preaching, and to the salvation of souls. In a word, we can say that theology was a fundamentally *spiritual* discipline. When Aquinas composed the *ST*, he was overtly aware of the obligations that attended his reception of this sacred office. Thus, the *ST* arises from the profound depths of who Aquinas was as a person.

Aquinas was not only a theologian, of course. He was also a philosopher of the first order. Throughout his academic career, he consistently turned his attention to questions and issues that confounded the greatest scientists and philosophers of his day. His commentaries on the writings of Aristotle, for example, reveal his prodigious acuity in the order of reason and natural reality. Even now, Aquinas's philosophical writings remain precious resources for those who wish to understand the natural order of things.

The *ST*, however, reflects Aquinas's commitment to sacred truth. Truth is the conformity of the mind to reality—knowledge of the way things actually are in themselves. There are two types of truth: *naturally knowable truths* and *divine truths*. Naturally knowable truths are those truths accessible to human observation and reflection. They lie within the grasp of unaided human reason.

Divine truths, by contrast, lie beyond the reach of unaided human reason. No human person can grasp supernatural truths by their own observation, reflection, or ingenuity. Such truths originate from the sublimity of the infinite God. Consequently, human persons can only learn such truths if God reveals them. These truths include the mysteries of the Trinity, the Incarnation, and the sacraments. Only if God reveals these supernatural and divine truths can human persons arrive at some understanding of their content and meaning.

Contrary to contemporary sentiments, Aquinas did not consider the possibility of truth to be something suspect or elusive. Like most thirteenth-century persons, he realized that the truth was available to all. Admittedly, some persons enjoy a greater proficiency in intellectual matters than others. Nonetheless, all human persons are fundamentally inclined to the truth. Knowledge of the truth is not something reserved for an elite few, nor is the truth fabricated by an influential corporate body. Rather, the truth reflects the outward orientation of the human person. From a very young age, human persons are curious about the way things are. They want to know the answers to many questions: *What is that? How does that work? Why does that behave in this manner?* It is critically important for everyone to understand the nature of reality. Just as all need food and drink in order to live, so all require truth in order to thrive. All of us are fundamentally ordered to the truth, and therefore knowledge of the truth lies within the reach of each and every person.

This dynamic also applies to divinely revealed truths. Although divine truths exceed the empirical proof and intellectual comprehension of human creatures, such truths are still—really and truly—knowable. Indeed, as we will see in subsequent chapters, divinely revealed truths are the *truest* truths. Why? Because our knowledge of these truths comes from God himself—the source of all truth. God is truth. And he can neither suffer nor cause error. God cannot act in a way contrary to his very being and identity. Because God is truth, God only does true things.

The *ST* is a book written by a Teacher of Catholic truth. It is not a work of mere opinions or hypotheses. Quite the contrary, the *ST* reflects Aquinas's conviction that the human person can actually understand and contemplate the sacred mysteries that God reveals out of love. Hence, there is nothing tentative about the *ST*'s nature, purpose, and goal. It is a work that glories in the goodness of God and celebrates the capacities of the human person. God reveals his precious mysteries to human persons—in a way that they can receive. And human persons, by his design, are capable of receiving God's precious mysteries and of consecrating their lives to these sacred realities.

The Instruction of Beginners

Aquinas explains that the Teacher of Catholic truth has a pedagogical obligation not only to students who already possess a facility in divine things (the "proficient") but also to those who are just starting out (the "beginners"). Invoking St. Paul's own example of forming "little ones in Christ" on a metaphorical diet of "milk to drink, not meat" (1 Cor 3:1–2), Aquinas explains that the *ST* is ordered to the formation of "novices" who are just commencing their study of sacred things. Aquinas's intended readers, thus, are beginners who seek to understand who God is and what God does.

The title "beginner" requires some clarification, however. Anyone who picks up the *ST* and reads these opening lines is, perhaps, consoled to hear that Aquinas intends to provide an introductory overview of Christian theology. Often, this consolation quickly cedes to confusion and frustration. As readers advance through the *ST*, they quickly encounter terminology, modes of writing, and nuanced conclusions that strike them as anything but introductory or suitable for beginners.

Who, exactly, are the "beginners" that Aquinas has in mind? For centuries scholars have debated the exact identity of Aquinas's audience. What all agree upon, however, is that Aquinas is writing for a very specific kind of novice. He is not writing for beginners who have never engaged in advanced studies. Rather, he is writing for beginners in divine things. These are beginners in what we can call Christian theology, but they are most certainly not beginners when it comes to other disciplines—especially philosophy. Aquinas presupposes that his beginning theology students already possess some formation in philosophy.

What is philosophy? Philosophy is the study of reality—of all that exists. Specifically, it is the study of reality by means of human reason.[2] The goal of philosophy is to arrive at wisdom—knowledge not merely of facts or phenomena, but of the order of things in light of reality's highest principles.[3] This is why Aquinas reasonably assumed that his readers, beginning their study of sacred doctrine, would already possess some proficiency in philosophy. We cannot adequately begin to understand divine reality—in an ordered and precise manner—unless we first understand something about natural reality.

In order to illustrate this point, we recall that God has revealed to us a sacred mystery: "Take and eat; this is my body" (Mt 26:26). Jesus reveals that Holy Communion is nothing less than his Sacred Body. We would not be able to know that Holy Communion is the true Body and Blood of Christ unless he revealed this truth to us. Why? No amount of scientific or rational scrutiny can demonstrate or verify the Real Presence of Jesus in the Eucharist. The Real Presence is not evident to human reason. It is evident to divine reason, however. And God has deigned to share this truth with us—a truth evident to him (even if not evident to us).

Philosophy does not have access to the divinely revealed mysteries of the faith. These mysteries, by definition, exceed the limits of naked human reason. Nonetheless, philosophy is important for understanding what God divinely reveals. Jesus has said that "this is my body." But if we do not properly understand what "is" means—what it means "to be," what being is in itself—then we will not be able to grasp fully what it means to say that Holy Communion *is* the Body of Christ. And this is why philosophy is necessary for the study of theology. How we understand natural reality will shape how we understand divine reality.

Although philosophy is certainly not sacred theology, philosophy is inescapably relevant to sacred theology. All of our presuppositions and fundamental convictions about being and reality will shape how we understand divine revelation. Thus, for the theologian, it is not so much a question of whether or not one will have philosophical presuppositions. Rather, the real question is whether or not one will have good and sound philosophical presuppositions.

The medieval Teachers of Catholic truth recognized the ineluctable importance of philosophy for the study of theology. And this is why students of theology were not able to enroll in courses of theology without extensive philosophical preparation. Even today, Catholic seminaries require that seminarians take a few years of preparatory philosophical courses before beginning their theological studies.

Thus, the "beginners" for whom Aquinas writes in the *ST* are beginners in the study of sacred doctrine. They are not absolute beginners, however. They have already undergone a rigorous philosophical preparation for the study of the divine mysteries. Aquinas's intended readers in the *ST* are beginners in theology but not beginners in philosophy.

Perhaps not all of us have had the opportunity to study philosophy. This should not discourage us, however. One of my tasks in this book is to provide supplementary philosophical guidance as we follow Aquinas in his presentation of Christian doctrine. We must recognize, however, that readers who benefit fully from the theological riches of the *ST* have devoted time to the serious study of philosophy—whether they be readers from the thirteenth or the twenty-first century.

The above reflections on the philosophical learning that Aquinas presupposes in his readers leads us to a humbling fact: No matter how wise or learned we might be in matters natural, we are still beginners in the study of sacred doctrine. "The wisdom of the world is foolishness in the eyes of God" (1 Cor 3:19). As essential and as irreplaceable as philosophy is, it pales in comparison to the divine truths that God reveals to us in faith. Even if readers have mastered the mysteries of the natural universe, they are only beginners—novices—before the supernatural mysteries.

Consequently, the theme of humility is present in the opening sentence of the *ST*. Aquinas writes for readers who recognize that their natural knowledge is insufficient for human fulfillment. There is, thus, nothing presumptuous about the study of God or of the *ST*. Each reader—indeed, each Christian—comes before the transcendent God with the realization that he or she does not possess a comprehensive knowledge of all that is. There is much about reality that even the wisest and the most learned human persons cannot know by their own native capacities or efforts.

This emphasis on humility, however, is also conjoined to profound magnanimity—"a greatness of soul." Aquinas explicitly categorizes his readers as novices in the presence of divine things. Nonetheless, he is confident that his readers can advance in their knowledge of God—even in their knowledge of the most sublime mysteries of God. How do we know this? *Aquinas would not have written the hundreds of pages composing the* ST *unless he believed that it was possible for human persons to know God.* God does not reveal sacred truths in vain. Aquinas did not compose the *ST* from a sentiment of despair. Quite the contrary. The *ST* is a book of immense hope and joy-filled aspiration: Even beginners, it proclaims, can know the truth about God.

The true knowability of God is a truth most precious to Aquinas. As a member of the Order of Preachers, he consecrated his life to the study and to the proclamation of the saving mysteries of the faith. And as a Teacher of Catholic truth, Aquinas is convinced that human persons can truly know—and love—divine things. The most divine thing, of course, is God himself.

The Christian Religion

In the opening sentence of the *ST*, Aquinas thus identifies himself as the Teacher of Catholic truth and those for whom he writes as "beginners" in the study of divine things. He concludes this sentence by identifying the context in which he and his readers will meet: "We purpose in this book to treat of whatever belongs to the Christian religion." In the *ST*, Aquinas and his readers, together, will devote their attention to *the Christian religion.*

"Religion" is not a favored phenomenon today. Quite commonly, religious matters are associated with artificial and empty customs. Religion is not considered to be something of essential importance. External religious practices are frequently disregarded. Indeed, contemporary persons frequently describe themselves as "spiritual but not religious." The spiritual life—as something fundamentally distinct from external locations, postures, or gestures—is regarded as essentially important to human flourishing. The reason for the prioritization of the spiritual life over one's religious identity lies in the fact that it is possible to perform religious practices without a consonant spiritual life. It is possible to participate in a religious service without actually believing in—or living according to—the most important spiritual truths. Religious dissimulation is a real phenomenon. Regrettably, people can "fake" religion.

Such disingenuous religious practices are not new. Aquinas himself was certainly aware that not all people "practiced what they preached." Moreover, he consistently emphasized the importance of a sincere and ardent spiritual life. As we will see, Aquinas was not only a philosophical and theological genius but also a spiritual master. The dynamics of the spiritual life reside at the heart of Aquinas's teaching.

But Aquinas also recognized that it is, ultimately, impossible to be spiritual but not religious. Why is this impossible? When human persons love someone or something in a wholehearted way, human persons love totally—this includes the body as well as the soul. For example, a couple on their wedding day do not merely intend to love each other in an exclusively "spiritual" way—they want to love each other completely. Physically and spiritually. They wish to reside together and to share everything with each other—even their very bodies. Because human persons are not just spiritual but also corporeal beings, they love completely in ways both spiritual and physical.

The same applies to our love for God. When we love God with the totality that he merits, we love him completely. We give him all of ourselves. Body and soul. Christian religious practices—like attending Mass on Sunday or making physical gestures like the Sign of the Cross—are inescapable parts of loving God with our whole selves.

We do not love God—or anyone, for that matter—with only our thoughts and affections. The entirety of our existence enters into our relationships with those whom we love most. And this is why the *ST* is intent on the Christian religion—not just Christian ideas. Although many nuanced precisions and abstract distinctions punctuate the *ST*, the focus of Aquinas's book is the complete transformation of his readers in Jesus Christ.

Our author is not interested in cultivating a class of smart people. Aquinas is not a disconnected intellectual. He is a man intent on holiness—on knowing and loving God with all of his being. And the *ST* is the context in which his readers can learn how to love God spiritually and religiously. Thus, Aquinas signals that his goal in the *ST* is to provide a holistic account of who God is, what God does, and how God transforms the entirety of his beloved children. The *ST* sets out to treat all things that pertain to following Christ and to living in union with him. Everything that is pertinent to the Christian religion is relevant to the *ST*—and important for Aquinas and his readers. Again, the *ST* is not a book that summarizes ideas. The *ST* is a book in which Aquinas and his readers study who God is and what we are in God.

To be a teacher of Catholic truth is not merely to be a professor who informs the mind. The Christian religion touches on all aspects of human life. And the *ST*, thus, is ordered to much more than information. It is intent on life transformation. Salvation.

Things That Frustrate the Instruction of Beginners

After Aquinas has identified himself, his intended readers, and what he plans to teach his readers, he pauses to identify common obstacles that frequently impede the effective instruction of beginners. Aquinas was aware that learning divine truth is not easy. Moreover, he regretted that sincere students were often frustrated in their study of sacred doctrine. Thus, he points to several impediments that characterized the theological formation of his day.

> We have considered that novices in this doctrine have often been hampered by what they have found written by various authors, partly on account of the multiplication of useless questions, articles, and arguments; partly also because the things such novices need to know are not taught according to the order of the discipline, but according as was needed for commenting on books, or according as an opportunity for raising a disputed question presented itself; partly, too, because frequent repetition of the same things brought weariness and confusion to the minds of the readers. (*ST*, Prologue)

Aquinas wrote the *ST* because he believed that other books and documents were not properly suited for the pedagogical needs of beginning students. He wanted his book to be different—to be a supremely useful work.

Aquinas does not deny that there were valuable theological texts before he wrote the *ST*. Even a cursory glance at Aquinas's writings reveals that he held other theological authors in the highest regard. Throughout the *ST*, he regularly cites with deference and appreciation other theological authors, especially the church fathers. Rather, his point is that other theological books were not written in a way suited for the instruction of beginners. Other books may say true, profound, and beautiful things about God and the things of God, but they were not written with the specific needs of beginning students at the forefront of their design. Critically, students were "not taught according to the order of discipline"—the order of teaching and learning.

Aquinas observes that many books were not written strictly for pedagogy but often for other motivations, such as commentating. Commentaries on sacred and theological texts were a prominent part of thirteenth-century theology. At that time, in order to become a master in theology, advanced students (called "bachelors") had to write a long commentary on an influential twelfth-century work called the *Sentences*, written by Peter Lombard. Once these students had completed their *Sentences* commentary, they became a "master" teacher of theology. Masters in theology were those professors qualified to occupy a chair of theology in the university setting.

The work of the master in theology was also, largely, commentarial.[4] Although masters did not lecture on the *Sentences* of Peter Lombard, their classroom instruction consisted of an extended commentary on the Bible. As a master in theology, Aquinas himself fulfilled this task of expositing the scriptures in the university setting. Indeed, his commentaries on numerous books of the Bible come from his classroom lectures.[5]

Aquinas, of course, like all Christians, held the Bible in highest regard. The Bible is divinely inspired by the Holy Spirit—it is nothing less than the written Word of God. Even so, he recognized that reading commentaries on the scriptures is not always the most effective way to learn sacred theology. The reason for this is that the Bible is not a single book—it is a series of books. The sacred scriptures did not fall from heaven in a single volume. The books of the Bible were composed by many inspired authors across thousands of years. And the books collected in the Bible reflect different historical periods, literary genres, and audiences. The Bible is not a systematic presentation of the Christian religion. This fact in no way denigrates the sanctity of the scriptures. Rather, this observation merely points out that the Bible is not a theological textbook.[6] And Aquinas believed that beginning students required a "summary" (*summa*) of the whole of Christian theology in order to appreciate the inspired books found in the Bible. In short, Aquinas believed that the Bible is more fully understood by those who first understand the Christian religion.

After observing the pedagogical limitations of commentaries on books, our author also invokes one of the other professional tasks of thirteenth-century masters in theology: disputation. In addition to commenting on the Bible in the classroom, masters were also required to preside at formal theological discussions called "disputes." Theological disputes were a regular part of academic life. They consisted of organized debates between advanced students about diverse theological topics. In these disputes, the master would provide an authoritative determination about the truth after the students had offered their respective arguments. Just as Aquinas's biblical commentaries record his classroom instruction, his various *Disputed Questions* record his participation in this aspect of university life.

These formal disputations were valuable insofar as they provided audiences with deep and intricate examinations of various theological topics and questions. To this day, Aquinas's numerous *Disputed Questions* remain important resources for theologians who wish to delve deeper into Aquinas's thought on different topics.[7] The disputations are stunning examples of high-level theological discourse.

Aquinas understandably recognized, however, that these disputations were not suitable for the instruction of beginners. Although often focused on specific theological topics, they did not proceed in an organic or systematic way that aligned with the order of teaching and learning. A variety of arguments and nuances were often introduced during the course of a disputation. Often, these arguments and nuances lacked systematic cohesion or natural development—both essential to effective pedagogy. In sum, disputations were suited to more advanced students in theology, not to beginners.

Thus, Aquinas is intent in the *ST* to avoid things that impede theological instruction: "the multiplication of useless questions, articles, and arguments," as well as the "frequent repetition of the same things"—experiences that can bring "weariness and confusion to the minds of the readers." By explicit design, the *ST* is neither a commentary nor a collection of scattered disputations. Rather, the *ST* is designed to address the things beginning students "need to know." The essential truths of the Christian religion are the key elements of the *ST*. Moreover, these essential truths will not be presented according to the rather desultory order that commentaries and disputations frequently foster. Aquinas promises his readers that he will strictly follow the "order of discipline"—that is, an order that is best suited for teaching and learning.

This strict and precise order of teaching and learning informs the *ST*. As we will see in future chapters, the structure of the *ST*—as a literary whole and in each of its discrete parts—is one of its most significant characteristics. In fact, the book's outline is almost as important as what Aquinas discusses in a particular passage. There is nothing capricious about the pedagogical progression that readers find in the *ST*: Everything is organized so as to render the mysteries of the Christian religion intelligible to readers.

Consequently, the *ST* is best regarded as a unified whole. It is meant to be studied from beginning to end. Although it is, of course, useful to consult what the *ST* says in a single section, readers cannot derive the full value of the *ST* by reading it in a piecemeal fashion. Aquinas intended each subsequent section of the *ST* to build upon the previous sections. The meticulously formulated structure of the *ST* is really the key to understanding each of the work's respective parts. We will pay close attention to the order of the *ST* in the pages that follow.

The *Summa Theologica*: A Work of Grace

Aquinas concludes his prologue to the *ST* with an important closing sentence:

> Endeavoring to avoid these and other like faults, we shall try, trusting in God's help, to set forth whatever belongs to Sacred Doctrine as briefly and clearly as the matter itself may allow. (*ST*, Prologue)

Aquinas promises his readers that he will strive to avoid the pedagogical weaknesses associated with commentaries and disputations. The *ST* will be structured around the educational requirements of his readers. Thus, brevity and clarity are of shaping importance in his presentation of sacred doctrine. Aquinas intends the *ST* to be a work of both concision and precision. There is to be nothing superfluous or irrelevant in his masterpiece. Only those things essential to the Christian religion will be treated in this work—and these essential things will be presented in a way suited to the needs of beginners.

We pause here to call attention to a significant detail—nestled in the very center—of this concluding sentence: Aquinas invokes *divine assistance* as he begins this new project. For those not yet familiar with the contents of the *ST*, Aquinas's confidence in "God's help" may appear to be the tender invocation of a pious priest. Indeed it is, and indeed he was. But this reference to divine assistance also carries with it profound implications. As we will see when we consider the middle of the *ST* in later chapters of this book, "divine help" is another way of referring to God's causal influence on his creatures—moving and directing them according to divine wisdom and love. Aquinas entrusts himself to the *grace* of God as he begins his summary of sacred doctrine.

None of those who knew Aquinas described him as melodramatic. He was known for being a measured, recollected, and deliberate man.[8] His invocation of divine help, thus, originates from his conviction that he stood in need of something more than his own native ingenuity in order to fulfill the task proposed in the *ST*. Aquinas recognized that the realization of his vision for the *ST* exceeded his own resources—and that he would be unable to achieve it without the grace of God.

Other theologians have written large books throughout history, some even longer than the *ST*. Aquinas himself was accustomed to writing long texts. The expected length of the *ST* is not what intimidated Aquinas. The thing that made Aquinas pause to invoke divine help before he launched into this project was its *revolutionary* nature. The *ST* was to be something unprecedented.

As we saw earlier in this chapter, Aquinas identifies various things that frustrate the theological formation of beginners. What is implicit in these observations, however, is this unavoidable conclusion: *Aquinas was convinced that the normal course of theological studies was not entirely effective*. Otherwise put, the university program of theological studies was not fully successful. Aquinas did not think that his professional activities as a master in theology—lecturing on the Bible and participating in public disputations—were meeting the needs of his students. The official program of academic theology, itself, required rethinking and restructuring. The very existence of the *ST* amounts to something like a subtle indictment of the academic life in which he was a celebrated participant.

The *ST*'s prologue reveals that Aquinas was attentive to the students that he encountered in his classroom and in his disputations. It also shows that he was convinced that his students needed something different than what they were customarily receiving in their formal theological studies. This helps to emphasize how unique the *ST* truly was in the thirteenth century. The *ST* was a work that would not quite fit into the ordinary practice of Christian theology at the time. Hence, it is unsurprising that Aquinas did not teach from the *ST* in the classroom.[9]

Moreover, Aquinas composed the *ST* in addition to his professorial responsibilities in the academic classroom and in the disputation hall. He was so convicted about the need for a new, different approach to Christian instruction that he assumed the burden of composing a radically different type of work—a work that had no immediate place in his professional life.

The *ST* is nothing short of prophetic. Aquinas was writing for students who would benefit from his book in future years. Although there were other theological *summae* composed before and after the *ST*, Aquinas's *summa* remains unique because of its synthetic, comprehensive, and formally pedagogical character. The needs of students—the *order of teaching and learning*—are foundational to the *ST* and consistently inform its structure and method.

The *ST* was eventually adopted as a standard, primary textbook for the study of sacred doctrine. But this adoption did not take place in Aquinas's own lifetime; rather, it took several decades for the *ST* to be included in theological curricula. This delay, we assume, would not have surprised Aquinas. The *ST*'s prologue signals his awareness of the unique nature of this new work.

And as Aquinas confided himself to divine help when he set out to compose the *ST*, we likewise entrust ourselves to divine grace as we begin to study this incredible labor of love and generosity. No one can contemplate the mysteries of God without God's help. Thankfully, God always assists those who seek to know and to love him. And Aquinas's *ST* is one of the most overt examples of God's help for students of sacred theology.

Perhaps Aquinas did not foresee, exactly, how influential his *ST* would be in the history of Christian doctrine. Nonetheless, given the fact that he wrote the *ST* with the needs of beginners in mind, it is not much of an exaggeration to conclude: *Aquinas was writing for us*.

CHAPTER 2

The Parts of the *Summa Theologica*

The *ST* is a single book. It is also a meticulously envisioned, carefully constructed, and precisely executed book. As we saw in the previous chapter, Aquinas was exquisite in the deliberation with which he fashioned and ordered every element the *ST*. The book contains no wasted space or extraneous material. Every detail contributes to Aquinas's pedagogical goal: to provide a holistic overview of "Catholic truth."

Because of what we might call the *ST*'s literary intricacy, the book comprises many moving parts through which readers advance. Beginning readers, thus, can find it difficult to navigate the various sections of the *ST*. In order to demystify the structure and method of the *ST*, this chapter will summarize how the *ST* "works," so to speak, as a literary whole.

The Division of the *Summa Theologica*

We can diagram the literary components of the *ST* as shown on the following page.

Thus, the *ST* is a unified book—a unified book divided into three *parts*. Each part of the *ST* contains various *treatises* that address broad theological topics. Each treatise is made up of a series of *questions* that consider specific theological topics. Each question consists of a series of *articles* that consider precise questions related to the specific theological topics of the respective question. Finally, each article comprises *objections*, a *sed contra* ("On the contrary"), a *response*, and *replies* to the objections of the article.

The Parts of the *Summa Theologica*

The three parts of the *ST* are usually referred to by their Latin titles. The first part of the *ST* is called the *Prima pars* (pronounced "pree-muh pahrz"). The second part is called the *Secunda pars* (pronounced "suh-cuhn-duh pahrz"). The third part is called the *Tertia pars* (pronounced "tuhr-zee-uh pahrz").

Although both the *Prima pars* and the *Tertia pars* are single parts, the *Secunda pars* is divided into two sub-parts—the *Prima secundae pars* (pronounced "pree-mah secuhn-day pahrz") and the *Secunda secundae pars* (pronounced "secuhn-duh secuhn-day pahrz"), respectively. The *Prima secundae* (*pars*) means "the first of the second (part)" of the *ST*. The *Secunda secundae* (*pars*) means "the second of the second (part)."

In many editions of the *ST*, there is also an additional "*Supplementum*" (pronounced "suh-pleh-mehn-toom") that comes after the *Tertia pars*. Aquinas died before he completed the final part of the *ST*, the *Tertia pars*. Thus, this "Supplement" follows the trajectory of the third part and attempts to supply what Aquinas's students believed he would have written

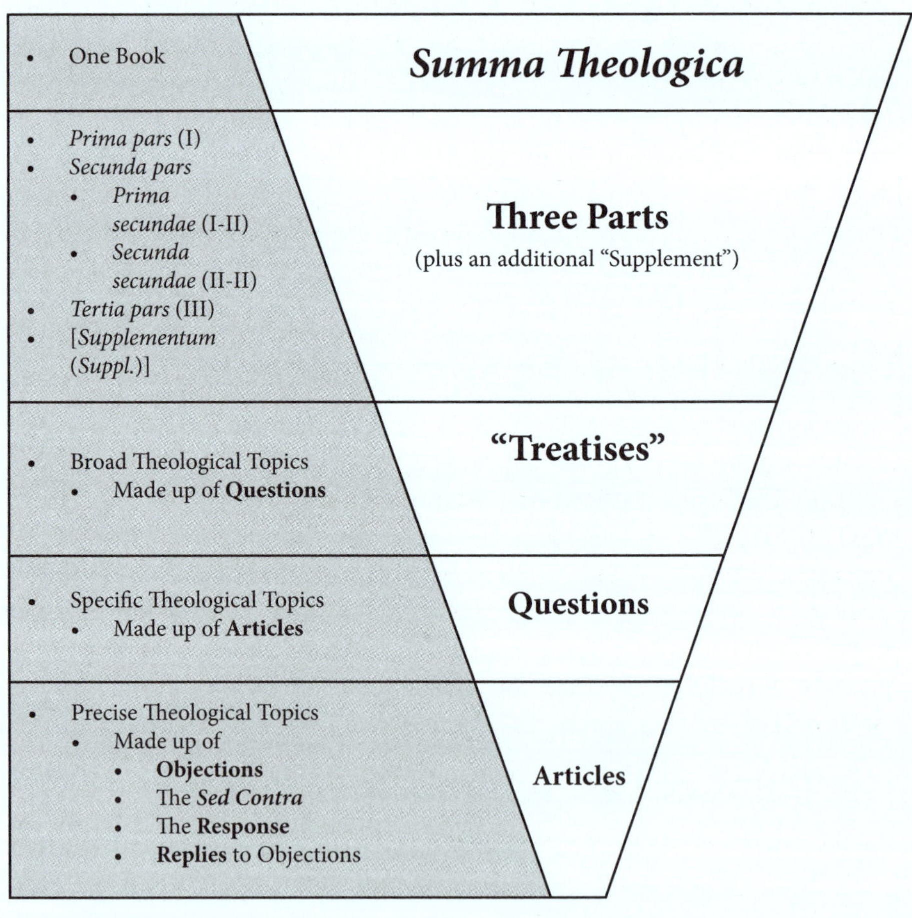

had he lived to finish the *ST*. The *Supplementum* was added by Aquinas's disciples.[1] It is largely drawn from Aquinas's earlier writings (specifically, his youthful commentary on the *Sentences* of Peter Lombard). Although the *Supplementum* is a useful text, it is generally not regarded as a definitive expression of Aquinas's thought (certainly not of his mature thought).

When authors cite the *ST*, they customarily employ the following abbreviations:

Summa Theologica Abbreviations

Summa Theologica	*ST* (or *STh*)
The ***Prima pars*** (the first part)	I
The ***Prima secundae pars*** (the first part of the second part)	I-II
The ***Secunda secundae pars*** (the second part of the second part)	II-II
The ***Tertia pars*** (the third part)	III
The ***Supplementum*** (a supplemental addition to the third part, added after Aquinas's death)	*Suppl.*
Prologue	prol.
Question	q. (pl. qq.)
Article	a. (pl. aa.)
Objection	obj.
Sed contra	s.c.
Reply to Objection	ad
"namely"	viz.

The Roman numerals employed in the above chart (e.g., I, I-II, et al.) are the most common ways of referring to the respective parts of the *ST*. (Sometimes, the *Prima pars* is abbreviated as "Ia," the *Prima secundae* as "IaIIae," the *Secunda secundae* as "IIaIIae," and the *Tertia pars* as "IIIa.")

Thus, the reference "*ST* I, q. 2, a. 3" is an abbreviated way of saying "*Summa Theologica*, *Prima pars*, question two, article three." Another example would be "*ST* I-II, q. 5, a. 2, obj. 3." This is an abbreviated form of "*Summa Theologica*, *Prima secundae pars*, question five, article two, objection three." "*ST* III, q. 6, a. 3, s.c." indicates "*Summa Theologica*, *Tertia pars*, question six, article three, the *sed contra*." And "*ST* III, q. 7, a. 2, ad 1" indicates "*Summa Theologica*, *Tertia pars*, question seven, article two, reply to objection one."

Treatises, Questions, and Articles

Each part of the *ST* contains *treatises*, *questions*, and *articles*. The essential distinction between the treatises, questions, and articles of the *ST* is the respective precision and focus of a given subject or topic. The *treatises* are recognized groupings of broader theological categories (e.g., *ST* I, qq. 2–26 is frequently referred to as the "Treatise on the One God"). Each treatise comprises discrete *questions* that address specific theological topics (e.g., *ST* I, q. 4: "The Perfection of God"). And each *article* examines a precise element of each question (e.g., *ST* I, q. 4, a. 2: "Whether God is perfect universally?").

As a general practice, Aquinas helpfully summarizes the content of a question in the beginning articles and in the concluding article(s). Thus, someone who wants to get a feel for what Aquinas is arguing would do well to briefly examine the early and the concluding articles of a given question.

In the *ST*, each question's article is made up of the following elements: a series of *objections*, a *sed contra*, a *response*, and *replies* to the series of objections. The *objections* present arguments for positions that Aquinas does *not* endorse. The *sed contra* (usually translated as "On the contrary") typically provides a concise citation, argument, or reason for the conclusion that Aquinas does endorse. The *response* (or "*respondeo*," usually translated as "I answer that") is generally the longest part of each article. In the response, Aquinas presents a series of arguments in support of the position he endorses. The response, thus, is the "heart" of each article. Indeed, the response is sometimes referred to as the "*corpus*" or the "body" of an article. Finally, after his response, Aquinas provides a series of *replies* to each of the arguments presented in the objections that come at the beginning of each article.

Many readers of the *ST* skip over the objections and jump straight to an article's *sed contra* or the response. Such a practice is certainly not harmful. The *sed contra* and the response express Aquinas's thought on a particular question. Nonetheless, Aquinas was the author of the entire *ST*. And each element of the *ST* bears his authorial influence. The objections, thus, are not incidental to the points that Aquinas makes in each article.[11] In brief, Aquinas intended that readers pay attention to the carefully crafted objections (and the replies to the objections). Again, there are no wasted or unnecessary elements of the *ST*. Every element of the *ST* has a pedagogical purpose.

Exceptionally, Aquinas will sometimes conclude an article by correcting the argument summarized in the *sed contra* (for example, see *ST* I, q. 17, a. 1). This is a rare occurrence. The *sed contra* is usually consistent with Aquinas's own thought as expressed in an article's response. But the *sed contra* does not always fully express Aquinas's conclusions about a particular matter.

Consequently, each article of the *ST* should be regarded as an integral whole. The most thorough way of reading the *ST* would be to read each article from beginning to end—reading from the first objection all the way through the reply to the final objection. This approach ensures that readers proceed through an article in the way that Aquinas intended.

An Interpretive Key: The Prologues of the *Summa Theologica*

As we progress through this book, the importance of the various prologues that introduce the parts, treatises, and questions of the *ST* will become quite evident. These (usually short) introductions are of utmost importance for understanding the logic, order, and unity that inform the *ST*. The prologues provide the guidelines for how each topic fits into the *ST* as a whole. Moreover, these prologues explain why a given subject or doctrine is treated in a particular place. As noted earlier, the order of the treatises and questions is almost as important as the specific points that Aquinas makes in a given passage of the *ST*.

Although readers who wish to benefit from the *ST* do not have to read the work from beginning to end, this approach is certainly the one that Aquinas had in mind. The *ST* is akin to a snowball—each section presupposes and builds upon previous sections. And the key thing to keep in mind is that *Aquinas generally identifies the most important principles at the beginning of a treatise or question.* Thus, it would be beneficial, at a minimum, to read the initial articles at the beginning of a question before advancing to subsequent sections. This method provides readers with a foundational grasp of the most important concepts.

In short, it is not necessary to read the *ST* all the way through in order to benefit from Aquinas's wisdom—but only such an approach can bestow that wisdom in its fullness.

CHAPTER 3

Sacred Doctrine

(ST I, q. 1)

As we saw in our first chapter, Aquinas crafted the *ST* with the utmost care. In our second chapter, we observed that each section of the *ST* presupposes and builds upon previous sections. Thus, it is of the highest importance that he begins the *ST* with a consideration of *sacred doctrine* (*sacra doctrina*, "holy teaching" in Latin), that is, divinely revealed knowledge. Indeed, this topic—the explicit topic of the very first question of the *ST*—is essential for all that follows.

We recall Aquinas's "purpose" (*intentio*, in Latin) from the *ST*'s general prologue: "to treat of whatever belongs to the Christian religion in such a way as may befit the instruction of beginners." He returns to this authorial intention in the prologue to the *ST*'s first question: "To place our purpose within proper limits, we first endeavor to investigate the nature and extent of this sacred doctrine" (*ST* I, q. 1, prol.).

Because precision and clarity characterize the *ST*, Aquinas points to the governing importance of the "nature and extent of this sacred doctrine." As this work is a "summary" of theology, its shape and content depend in an essential way upon the nature of sacred doctrine. Consequently, the entire *ST* proceeds from what Aquinas explains in the *ST*'s opening question. All of the topics considered in subsequent questions fall within the ambit of sacred doctrine. The meaning of sacred doctrine establishes what, precisely, the *ST* examines—and the reason for the examination.

In brief, if we understand what sacred doctrine is and why it is important, then Aquinas's process in the proceeding sections of the *ST* will make sense. If we do not appreciate the nature and necessity of sacred doctrine, then we will be frustrated in our quest to grasp the shape and structure of Aquinas's presentation of this doctrine.

The Necessity of Sacred Doctrine

Aquinas begins the *ST* by asking: *Is sacred doctrine necessary?* (*ST* I, q. 1, a. 1). Starting with the absolute necessity of sacred doctrine may perplex us. Why does he feel the need to justify the necessity of sacred doctrine? He begins with this question for a very important reason: The entire *ST* is a work ordered to the exposition of sacred doctrine. If sacred doctrine were not necessary, then the *ST* itself would be a futile and useless project. Conversely, if sacred doctrine is necessary, then the utility of the *ST* is undeniable.

Aquinas is unambiguous in his conclusion: "It was necessary for man's salvation that there should be a knowledge revealed by God besides philosophical science built up by human reason." He justifies the necessity of sacred doctrine by way of two reasons. The first reason is *absolute*: Humans are ordered to God as to a supernatural end. The second reason is *relative*: It is difficult for humans to discover truths about God that are accessible by human reason.

With regard to the first reason, Aquinas quotes Isaiah 64:3 and explains that "man is directed to God, as to an end that surpasses the grasp of his reason." God is the term, the goal, the destination of the human person; and "the end must first be known by men who are to direct their thoughts and actions to the end." Aquinas concludes, "Hence it was necessary for the salvation of man that certain truths which exceed human reason should be made known to him by divine revelation." Because human salvation is absolutely important, sacred doctrine is absolutely necessary.

Humans need to foreknow an end, a destination, a goal in order to direct their thoughts, intentions, and actions to that end, destination, or goal. Although sacred doctrine is primarily about God, human action is a critically important element within sacred doctrine. Through human actions, the human person is ordered "to the perfect knowledge of God in which consists eternal bliss" (*ST* I, q. 1, a. 4). Because God is our supernatural end—and heaven our supernatural goal—we can only act in this life in a way directed to God through some foreknowledge, some pre-awareness, of what this supernatural goal actually is and what it requires of us and our actions. Thus, the human person requires from

God a kind of knowledge that is beyond the natural discovery of human reason. This knowledge comes directly and necessarily from God. Sacred doctrine comes *from* God and is directed *to* God. God is our salvation. And God reveals to us the way to our supernatural end: God himself.

Knowledge and Action

Why is knowledge so important for human life? Human nature is a *rational* nature. Consequently, authentically human action is rational action. Deliberate choices, conscious actions, and intentional goals shape human actions and human lives. The most important and defining actions of human life are not incidental or accidental in nature. The actions that characterize us most profoundly are those actions that we *intend* to do.

There is an essential difference between *accidentally* hitting someone standing next to us—whom, perhaps, we didn't see—and *deliberately* striking another person. Likewise, no one "accidentally" draws near to God. Deep friendship with God grows out of our profoundest desires and decisions. Thus, in order for human persons to live for God and to act in a way that conforms us to him, human persons must know who God is and what kinds of actions are consonant with him.

In order to draw nearer to God, we must know what God is like so that we can act accordingly.

The Relative Necessity of Sacred Doctrine

With regard to the second, *relative* reason for sacred doctrine's necessity, Aquinas observes that some truths about God are accessible to human reason. The most evident example of this kind of naturally knowable truth about God is the fact that God exists. It is possible for human reason to discover that God exists by reasoning from God's *effects*—the character of the things that God has created. Additionally, human reason can discover other important truths about God: for example, that there is only one God, that he is all-knowing and all-powerful, and so on. Nonetheless, Aquinas also observes that not all people possess the time, talent, or resources that would enable them to discover these naturally knowable truths about God.

Thus, although human reason can discover some essential truths about God, most human persons are not capable of engaging in the type of reasoning process that would enable them, personally, to demonstrate these essential truths.

Because knowledge about God is essentially important for human happiness and salvation, God has revealed who he is to the human persons he has called to himself. God does not want anyone to be ignorant about him or about his truth and his love. Salvation does not depend upon human resources or talents.

In sum, the human need for God lies at the heart of the human need for sacred doctrine. Human salvation requires knowledge revealed by God, divine revelation. Sacred doctrine is this divinely revealed knowledge. Therefore, sacred doctrine is necessary for human salvation.

The Nature of Sacred Doctrine

After Aquinas has justified the necessity of sacred doctrine, he proceeds to explore the nature of this doctrine. In the second article of *ST* I, q. 1, Aquinas considers whether sacred doctrine is a science. "Science" (or *scientia*) in Aquinas's lexicon differs in significant ways from our contemporary notions of scientific matters. For Aquinas, precisely speaking, a science is a unified discipline from which certain conclusions are drawn from *first principles*, the first and foundational truths of a given science. And it is precisely with regard to first principles that the initial difficulty of sacred doctrine's scientific status is called into question.

The Scientific "Problem" of Sacred Doctrine

Sciences such as physics and arithmetic are founded on first principles that are within the grasp of natural human discovery and inquiry. Sacred doctrine, however, is a discipline ordered to God toward a supernatural end that exceeds the native grasp of human resources and capacities. Thus, it is not immediately evident how sacred doctrine qualifies as a science when the essential starting points of this science—first principles beyond immediate human access—are not self-evident. Therefore, Aquinas must be able to explain how sacred doctrine can truly be a science when, by definition, sacred doctrine exceeds natural human capacities.

Aquinas reminds his readers that there are two kinds of science. The first kind of science proceeds from first principles discovered and known by the light of human understanding. The second type of science proceeds from first principles known through a higher science. Sacred doctrine is an example of this second type of science.

The first principles of sacred doctrine are known directly and immediately by God and by the saints. And God reveals to us these supernatural first principles. Therefore, although the principles are not self-evident to us, God has made them accessible to us. God makes principles that are self-evident to him accessible to us.

Through divine revelation, God communicates the first principles of sacred doctrine to us. And what are the first principles of sacred doctrine? Aquinas explains that the first principles of sacred doctrine are the *articles of faith* (*ST* I, q. 1, a. 7).

The Essence of Sacred Doctrine: Divine Revelation

God stands at the center of sacred doctrine. Whatever God has revealed falls under sacred doctrine *because God has revealed it*. God—as First Truth revealing—unites the science of sacred doctrine. This aspect of sacred doctrine—its "formal object"—is what accounts for all of sacred doctrine's characteristics. Because God is one, and the one God reveals saving truth, the saving truth is, likewise, one. Sacred doctrine is, preeminently, a unified science (*ST* I, q. 1, a. 3).

God also accounts for the nature of sacred doctrine as a *speculative* and a *practical* science. A speculative science is a science ordered, simply, to knowing the way things are. The end of speculative science is knowledge of the truth. A practical science is also ordered to the truth about reality. By contrast, practical sciences order truth to *action* or *operation*. In other words, practical sciences terminate in *applied truth* (for example, the science of medicine). Although sacred doctrine, uniquely, is a speculative and a practical science, Aquinas explains that sacred doctrine is primarily speculative "because it is more concerned with divine things than with human acts; though it does treat even of these latter, inasmuch as man is ordained by them to the perfect knowledge of God in which consists eternal bliss" (*ST* I, q. 1, a. 4).

All other practical sciences pale in comparison to sacred doctrine. Practical sciences are hierarchically classified according to the degree that they are ordered to a higher or to a more universal end. The end or purpose of sacred doctrine is all-exceeding: "eternal bliss." Heaven. Nothing is more elevated than this finality. All other sciences are inferior to sacred doctrine because their respective ends are incomplete in relation to beatific communion. Indeed, their respective ends are all subordinated to this one ultimate end. The end of sacred doctrine is, in truth, the ultimate end of every other practical science (*ST* I, q. 1, a. 5).

The Sublimity of Sacred Doctrine

Sacred doctrine is *noblest* of all the sciences because of the sublimity of its subject matter, the greatness of its certitude, and the ultimacy of its finality. Sacred doctrine transcends all other speculative sciences because its subject matter is superior—"this science treats chiefly those things which by their sublimity transcend human reason; while other sciences consider only those things which are within reason's grasp" (*ST* I, q. 1, a. 5). The sublimity of the subject matter arises from the supreme certitude of this science. The certainty of sacred doctrine is founded not in "the natural light of human reason, which can err." Rather, the certitude of sacred doctrine is founded "from the light of divine knowledge, which cannot be misled" (*ST* I, q. 1, a. 5).

The absolute sublimity of sacred doctrine explains why this doctrine is also, "absolutely," a *wisdom* (*ST* I, q. 1, a. 6). What is wisdom? Wisdom pertains to order and judgment. The wise man is the one who orders things properly, referring the lower in relation to the higher. The wise (or "sapiential") judgment of sacred doctrine is "acquired by study, though its principles are obtained by revelation" (*ST* I, q. 1, a. 7, ad 3). Sacred doctrine comprises the highest first principles. The sapiential character of sacred doctrine means that this doctrine enjoys the privilege of judging the principles of the other sciences (*ST* I, q. 1, a. 7, ad 2).

Wisdom is different, in an important way, from mere "intelligence." Intelligence proceeds in a horizontal manner (from a first to a second truth that is on the same plane of being as the first truth). Wisdom, in contrast, proceeds according to a vertical ordering (examining lower truths in light of higher truths). "Therefore he who considers absolutely the highest cause of the whole universe, namely God, is most of all called wise." Consequently, because "sacred doctrine essentially treats of God viewed as the highest cause . . . as far as He is known to Himself alone and revealed to others," Aquinas concludes that "sacred doctrine is especially called wisdom" (*ST* I, q. 1, a. 6). This doctrine enjoys the prerogative of ordering all of the other sciences—both in terms of principles and in terms of conclusions.[1]

The Subject of Sacred Doctrine: God

ST I, q. 1, a. 7 addresses the *subject* of sacred doctrine (sometimes translated, unfortunately, as "object").[2] Aquinas explains that the subject of a science is "that of which [a science] principally treats." In sacred doctrine, "the treatment is mainly about God; for it is called theology, as treating of God" (*ST* I, q. 1, a. 7, s.c.).

Of course, sacred doctrine treats of many things—even many things that are not God (e.g., the human person, virtue, vice, angels, demons, etc.). Nonetheless, "in sacred science, all things are treated under the aspect of God: either because they are God Himself or because they refer to God as their beginning and end" (*ST* I, q. 1, a. 7). As we have observed above, sacred doctrine is unified around God—the God who reveals his own sublime knowledge. Again, God-as-revealing is the essential aspect—the "formal object"—of sacred doctrine. Consequently, Aquinas warns his readers to keep the centrality of sacred doctrine's God-orientation prominent in their minds.

Sacred doctrine's formal object defines this divine science. Diverse topics fall within the scientific purview of sacred doctrine insofar "as they have reference to God"—insofar as they are *ordered* to God (*ST* I, q. 1, a. 7, ad 2). Thus, God himself is not the only topic that falls within the consideration of sacred doctrine. Indeed, all things can be considered in reference to divine revelation about God. We ought not confuse "what is treated of in this science" with "the aspect under which it is treated."

The Method of Sacred Doctrine

After expositing the nature of sacred doctrine, Aquinas then proceeds to consider the method of sacred doctrine. In other words, Aquinas turns his attention to the question: *How does sacred doctrine advance and operate as a science and wisdom? ST* I, q. 1, a. 8 outlines the *argumentative* character of sacred doctrine. Of course, here, "argumentative" does not mean disagreeable or combative, but rather *discursive*. An argument is a reasoned, logical, and certain progression from things known to things either unknown or less clearly known.

The starting points for this argumentative advancement within a science, of course, are the first principles of the science. Scientific first principles are the starting points of any science. No science ever outgrows its first principles. Moreover, no science argues for its first principles.

Rather, a science argues *from* its principles—first principles are the certain and reliable "starting points" for scientific development. Discursive advancement in a science always depends upon and presupposes its scientific first principles.

As we have already seen above, the first principles of sacred doctrine are the *articles of faith* (*ST* I, q. 1, a. 8). Aquinas explains the argumentative method of sacred doctrine thus: "From [the articles of faith, sacred doctrine] goes on to prove something else; as the Apostle from the resurrection of Christ argues in proof of the general resurrection (1 Cor. 15)" (*ST* I, q. 1, a. 8). From the first truths—the first principles—that God has revealed, the theologian is able to reason to other truths. Moreover, the conclusions drawn from these divinely revealed first principles participate in the certitude of the first principles themselves.

If one does not accept the articles of faith, scientific advancement is not possible. Why? The articles of faith—the first principles of sacred doctrine—are the irreplaceable starting points of the science. Thus, the theologian cannot truly "argue" with someone who denies the articles of faith—at least, not in a properly scientific manner.

Nonetheless, the theologian is never insecure before critics of the faith. "Since faith rests upon infallible truth, and since the contrary of a truth can never be demonstrated, it is clear that the arguments brought against faith cannot be demonstrations, but are difficulties that can be answered" (*ST* I, q. 1, a. 8). Thus, when dialoguing or reasoning with unbelievers, the theologian does not attempt to demonstrate the articles of faith—such a task would be at once foolish and impossible. Rather, the theologian answers the objections that are brought against the articles of the faith.

Because the truth of reason and the truth of faith never suffer contradiction—since God is the origin of both, and God cannot contradict himself—the theologian is never insecure before any objections. Sacred doctrine cannot prove its first principles. Nonetheless, it can show that its first principles are not contrary to the order of reason. The articles of faith neither contradict each other nor do they contradict the order of nature or of reason. Quite the contrary, the articles of faith excel the natural order of being and understanding. The first principles are not irrational. They are supra-rational.

Sacred Doctrine and the Language and Senses of Scripture

The final two articles of *ST* I, q. 1 examine certain peculiarities of sacred scripture that would seem to inveigh against sacred doctrine's scientific nature and requirements. Metaphorical speech and propositions with layers of meaning (i.e., the "senses" of scripture) would seem to contradict the scientific certitude of sacred doctrine. Why? A science cannot countenance ambiguity or equivocation.

Aquinas explains that sacred doctrine utilizes metaphors "as both necessary and useful" (*ST* I, q. 1, a. 9, ad 1). Metaphorical speech is both useful and necessary because of the requirements of human knowledge: "God provides for everything according to the capacity of its nature." All human knowledge "originates from sense" perception. Thus, "it is natural to man to attain to intellectual truths through sensible objects" (*ST* I, q. 1, a. 9). The Bible is one of the principal instruments of sacred doctrine. Thus, it is not inappropriate that divine revelation communicates "spiritual truths" to human persons in a way that fits their manner of understanding—"under the likeness of material things." It is important to recognize that Aquinas does not employ sacred doctrine and sacred scripture in an exactly identical way in the *ST*. Sacred scripture is a preeminent source of sacred doctrine, but sacred doctrine is not limited to the Bible. God's revelation preceded the composition and canonization of the Bible.

Metaphors do not contradict the purpose of sacred doctrine. Rather, they enable the human intellect to receive the divine truths communicated by sacred doctrine. Indeed, metaphors help to protect the human mind from error in accordance with the terrestrial knowledge of God, befitting those who are worthy to receive divine revelation (*ST* I, q. 1, a. 9, ad 3).

Likewise, God—as the first, inspiring author of the Bible—possesses the ability "to signify His meaning, not by words only (as man also can do), but also by things themselves" (*ST* I, q. 1, a. 10). Uniquely, as a divine science, sacred doctrine is able to communicate through both words and things. Thus, "the things signified by the words have themselves also a signification." Aquinas explains that the "first signification whereby words signify things belongs to the first sense, the historical or the literal." The "spiritual sense" is "based on" and "presupposes" this literal sense. All the senses of scripture "are founded on one—the literal [sense]—from which alone can any argument be drawn" (*ST* I, q. 1, a. 10, ad 1).

God is the author of all created reality. All things come from him. Thus, he is able to communicate divine truth not only through words but also through the very things signified by the words (see, for example, 1 Pt 3:19–22: Noah's Ark and Baptism). Sacred doctrine is informed by the Bible, whose text is not inimical to the scientific nature of the doctrine. God is the supernatural end of the human person, and he communicates divine truth to human persons in a way that they can really receive, profoundly contemplate, and discursively investigate.

Conclusion

In sum, Aquinas's presentation of sacred doctrine is salvific. It is contemplative. It is ordered to human holiness—transformative union with God. Sacred doctrine touches on all aspects of our humanity. Why? Because every part of our humanity is ordered to God, our supernatural end. The beatific vision is the destination of the human person, yes. But this supernatural finality can affect human living, human being, and human knowing and loving, on earth, even now. This is why God has revealed sacred doctrine to human persons.

And this is the office of St. Thomas Aquinas as the teacher of sacred theology, of Catholic truth and doctrine. He has to explain how God's truth shapes the lives of those who devote themselves to *faith seeking understanding*.

And this expository task is why Aquinas wrote the *ST*.

CHAPTER 4

The Structure of the *Summa Theologica*

It is difficult to overestimate the significance of the prologue to *ST* I, q. 2. Here, Aquinas reveals the fundamental structure of the *ST*:

> Because the chief aim of sacred doctrine is to teach the knowledge of God, not only as He is in Himself, but also as He is the beginning of things and their last end, and especially of rational creatures, as is clear from what has been already said, therefore, in our endeavor to expound this science, we shall treat: (1) Of God; (2) Of the rational creature's advance towards God; (3) Of Christ, Who as man, is our way to God. (*ST* I, q. 2, prol.)

The word "aim" (or *intentio*, in Latin) signals continuity with what Aquinas said in the general prologue to the *ST* and in the prologue to *ST* I, q. 1 (introducing sacred doctrine). This prologue to *ST* I, q. 2 unites Aquinas's authorial purpose (see chapter 1) with the doctrinal purpose or "intention" of sacred doctrine itself (see chapter 3). Unsurprisingly, when Aquinas explains the nature and characteristics of sacred doctrine, he emphasizes the fact that God is the subject of sacred doctrine (*ST* I, q. 1, a. 7). The *ST* is a book intent on the truth about God.

God is the supreme and unifying focus of the *ST*.

God and the "Intention" of Sacred Doctrine

The intention of sacred doctrine itself is clear: *to hand on knowledge about God*. This is its chief aim. And this knowledge about God is twofold: (1) it concerns God *in himself*, and (2) it concerns God *as he is the beginning and the end of all things*—especially as the beginning and end of rational creatures, such as human persons. As we noted in chapter 3, sacred doctrine is necessary for human salvation. Human salvation is the purpose of sacred doctrine. Therefore, human salvation is an essential consideration in an account of sacred doctrine.

In order to treat God, the subject of sacred doctrine, Aquinas explains that three things are necessary: (1) God; (2) the human person's movement, or advance, toward God; and (3) Jesus Christ who—"as man"—is our way of tending to God.

The *ST* bears this tripartite structure of sacred doctrine. The *ST* is a pedagogical instrument of sacred doctrine. Consequently, the *ST* itself reflects the subject of sacred doctrine. The *ST*'s broad division reflects this tripartite division of this holy teaching. We could, thus, provide the following as a preliminary outline of the *ST*:

- **Part I:** God (and what God does in creation)
- **Part II:** The Human Person's Movement Toward God (i.e., the "moral life")
- **Part III:** Jesus Christ (and the sacraments)

On one level, this division of the *ST* is accurate. Nonetheless, a question has perplexed *ST* readers for centuries: *Why does Aquinas place Jesus Christ in the third and final part of the* ST? In other words, *Why does Jesus come "last"?*

The reason for the perplexity of this detail is the fact that Jesus is "our way to God." Thus, would it not be more reasonable to consider Jesus *before* considering the human person's movement to God? Don't we need to know the "way" to God before we can understand how the human person advances through the way? Because Jesus is the means through which human persons are saved, would it not make more sense to examine the means itself before we examine what happens in those who undertake this means?

Aquinas, of course, was not oblivious to such sentiments. As we have already noted, he was keenly attuned to all of the details of the *ST*. Consequently, we can be certain that Aquinas had a good—and a pedagogically important—reason for situating Jesus in the third and final part of the *ST*. In order to recognize his reason for this arrangement, however, we have to pay close attention to other key prologues of the *ST*.

The Prologues and the Structure of the *ST*

As a good pedagogue, Aquinas helpfully summarizes an earlier part of the *ST* when he transitions to a subsequent part. It is in the *prologues* that Aquinas frequently explains the reasons behind the various steps in the *ST*. These prologues serve as contextualizing introductions to the different parts, treatises, and questions of his master work.

Of all of the *ST*'s prologues, one of the most significant is that which introduces the *Secunda pars*. This prologue is of central interpretative importance. Aquinas here summarizes what came before (in the *Prima pars*). He also explains how what came before flows naturally into what will follow (in the *Secunda pars*).

> Since, as [John] Damascene states (*De Fide Orth.* ii, 12), man is said to be made in God's image, in so far as the image implies "an intelligent being endowed with free-will and self-movement": now that we have treated of the exemplar, i.e. God, and of those things which came forth from the power of God in accordance with His will; it remains for us to treat of His image, i.e. man, inasmuch as he too is the principle of his actions, as having free-will and control of his actions. (*ST* I-II, prol.)

In this very precise sentence, Aquinas provides a concise account of two things: (1) the unifying principle of the *Prima pars*: "we have treated the exemplar, i.e., God" and (2) the unifying principle of the *Secunda pars*: "it remains for us to treat of His image, i.e., man."

God, the *exemplar*. Man, the *image of God*. These are the two *formalities* that make up the *ST*'s structure. And these two formalities prepare us for the answer to our question: Why does Aquinas examine Jesus last—in the *Tertia pars*?

The *Prima pars*: God—the "Exemplar"

Aquinas says that the *Prima pars* "treat[s] the exemplar, i.e., God." *Exemplarity* is the formality of the *ST*'s first part—the aspect under which all of the various topics comprising the *Prima pars* receive consideration. This formality of exemplarity originates in God himself: "God is the first exemplar cause of all things" (*ST* I, q. 44, a. 3).

What does it mean to say that God is the "exemplar" of all that is? An exemplar is the idea of something in the mind of an artist. Thus, an "exemplar" is a particular kind of idea in the mind of God: "a principle of making things" (*ST* I, q. 15, a. 3). Because God is the creator of all reality, he is the exemplar of all that is. God first *knows* what he will create before he actually creates it. Moreover, he establishes all that he creates within the order that he eternally envisioned.

As the creator of all contingent reality, God is the supreme and primary "artist" of all that is. Before an artist can create or fabricate something, however, the artist must have a conception of what he will make. For example, if I want to paint a portrait of my mother, I have to prepossess some conception of my mother, in my mind, before I apply paint to the canvas. This preconception—this idea or conception of my mother—is the exemplar.

Likewise, God has an idea of what he creates before he creates it. The natures of created things reflect God's goodness, his truth, and his order because these created things proceed from God's knowledge of them. Furthermore, God's knowledge is not really distinct from God's being. He is essentially one (*ST* I, q. 11). Thus, God does not simply possess exemplary knowledge in the divine intellect. He himself is the *exemplar* of all that he has created.

Aquinas considers many things in the *Prima pars* (e.g., God himself, creation, the angels, the human person). But each of these many things receive consideration under the light of *God's exemplarity*. Consequently, all of the things that Aquinas considers in the *Prima pars* are unified around God—God as the exemplar of all things (i.e., things that he has created).

Exemplarity is the unifying formality of the *ST*'s *Prima pars*; this unifying formality explains why and how Aquinas treats the distinct topics examined therein.

The *Secunda pars*: Man—the "Image of God"

Aquinas explains that *the human person as God's image—imago Dei*—is the formality that unifies the subjects investigated in the *Secunda pars*. Indeed, the principle of human persons as created in the image of God unifies each of the diverse topics considered in this part of the *ST*.

The formality of exemplarity is oriented around God. The formality of *image*, however, is oriented around the rational creature's reference to God. Thus, these two formalities enjoy deep consonance. Indeed, an image presupposes and reflects the shape of an exemplar. An image naturally follows from the exemplar. And an exemplar gives rise to images.

Although the *Secunda pars* of the *ST* considers numerous individual things and topics (e.g., man, human freedom, human action, grace, the virtues), each of these is only considered in reference to the formality of the human person as created in the image of God. All beings reflect God, the exemplar. Human persons, however, uniquely image who God is. In the prologue to the *Secunda pars*, Aquinas explains that creatures proceed "from the power of God in accordance with His will." The human person images God "inasmuch as he too is the principle of his actions, as having free-will and control of his actions." Humans actively reflect God's knowing and loving through their own acts of knowing and loving. God's rationality and freedom are imaged in the human person. Thus, the *imago Dei* expresses the fact that human creatures, as rational creatures, reflect the powers of knowing and loving that God eternally is (see *ST* I, q. 93, a. 4).

In sum, the *image of God* is the unifying formality of the *Secunda pars* of the *ST*. This formality follows naturally from the exemplar formality of the *Prima pars*. Images "exemplate"—reflect the exemplar—and the exemplar points to the image.

It is also important to note that the formality of divine exemplarity leads to—and, indeed, requires—the formality of the *image*. The *Prima pars* is ordered to the *Secunda pars*. Why? Exemplarity is not an absolutely independent notion. In other words, an exemplar is only an exemplar *of something*. Thus, the decision to structure the *ST* around the formalities of exemplarity and image reflects Aquinas's appropriation of the requirements of sacred doctrine itself: "as they have reference to God" (*ST* I, q. 1, a. 7, ad 2). God freely chose to create. He was under no obligation to do so. Thus, God can only be considered as an exemplar of creation *because* he has decided to create. And, because he has decided to create, human persons, uniquely, *image* their creator.

Sacred doctrine comes from God, but it is ordered to the salvation of human persons made in his image. The formality of exemplarity that unites the *Prima pars* leads to the formality of the image that unites the *Secunda pars*.

The *Tertia pars*: Jesus Christ—the Exemplar and the Image

If we return to the prologue to *ST* I, q. 2, we recall that Aquinas explains that the third part of the *ST* considers "Christ, Who as man, is our way to God." In the prologue to the *Tertia pars*, Aquinas explains that "it is necessary, in order to complete the work of theology, that after considering the last end of human life [*ST* I-II], and the virtues and vices [*ST* II-II], there should follow the consideration of the Savior of all, and of the benefits bestowed by Him on the human race." The *Tertia pars* focuses on Jesus Christ, the "Savior of all." The person and the work of Our Lord is the focus of the *ST*'s third part.

Aquinas then delineates the three elements that constitute the *Tertia pars*'s investigation of Jesus Christ, "the Savior of all": (1) "the Savior Himself," (2) "the sacraments by which we attain our salvation," and (3) "the end of immortal life to which we attain by the resurrection." (We recall, of course, that Aquinas died before he could complete the section on the sacraments and, thus, he never even began the section on immortal life.)

Jesus Christ stands at the center of the *Tertia pars*. Through Jesus we arrive at beatitude (i.e., the end of immortal life) by resurrection. And Jesus effects our movement toward this end through the sacraments. The Seven Sacraments of the Catholic Church are the instruments through which human persons—created in the image of God—are configured and conformed to Jesus (more about this in chapter 14).

The conjunction of the formality of exemplarity and the formality of the image of God explains why Aquinas's examination of Jesus is found in the third part of the *ST*. How so? Jesus Christ is both *the exemplar* (because he is God) and *the image* (because he is the Eternal Son) (*ST* III, q. 3, a. 8). Thus, the formality of the *Tertia pars* naturally follows from those of the *Prima pars* and of the *Secunda pars*, respectively. The *Tertia pars* presupposes and unites the exemplarity of the *ST*'s first part with the *imago Dei* dynamism of the second part. Jesus is the exemplar. Jesus is also *the* image—"the perfect image" (*ST* I, q. 88, a. 3). And Jesus assumed a human nature to save those made in the image of God according to God's exemplary knowledge.

Thus, the *Tertia pars* assumes within itself the formality of the *Prima pars* and the formality of the *Secunda pars* (see diagram below).

Conclusion

In sum, the exemplar-image *formalities* are the essential keys to understanding the fundamental structure of the *ST*. In the pages that follow, we will briefly examine what it means to examine the topics of the *Prima pars* under the aspect of God as exemplar and the topics of the *Secunda pars* under the aspect of the human person as created in the image of God. Moreover, we will also be able to recognize how both the exemplarity of the first part and the image of God aspect of the second part naturally culminate in an examination of Jesus Christ in the third part of the *ST*.

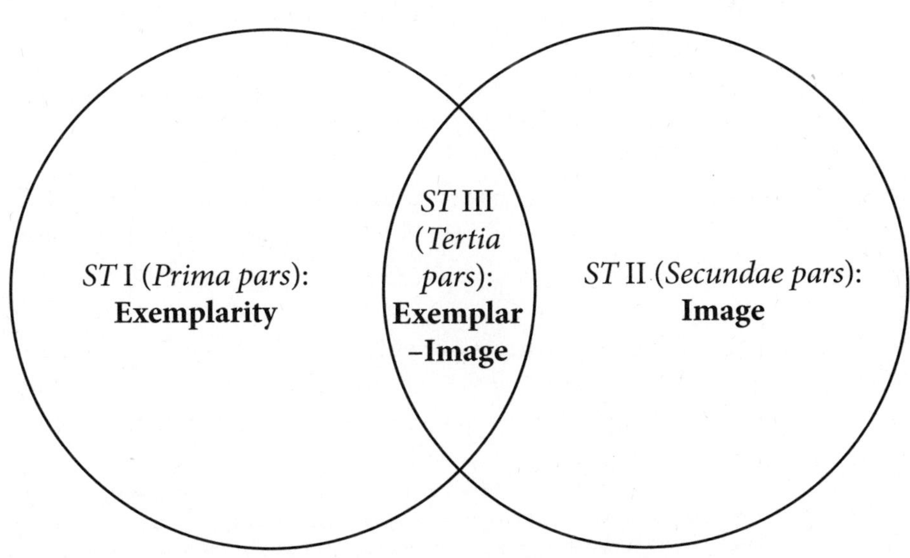

I. The First Part: God the Exemplar

Chapter 5

God as One and Three

(ST I, qq. 2–43)

In the prologue to the *ST* I, q. 1, Aquinas introduces the idea of sacred doctrine: "To place our purpose within proper limits, we first endeavor to investigate the nature and extent of this sacred doctrine." Aquinas provides a concise summary of sacred doctrine in ten articles. The remainder of the *ST* is his examination of the "extent" of sacred doctrine—literally, "those things to which sacred doctrine extends."

In chapter 4, we identified the structure of the *ST*. We saw that the *ST* proceeds according to two distinct but related formalities. The formality of *exemplarity* unites and governs the *Prima pars*. The formality of *image* unites and governs the *Secunda pars*. And the *Tertia pars*, which is centered on the person and work of Jesus Christ, assumes and unites the formalities of the first two parts because the Incarnate Word is both the exemplar and the image.

In chapter 1, we saw that the purpose of the *ST* is to present the content (i.e., the "matter") of sacred doctrine in a way that is suited to the needs of beginners. We also saw that, in order to avoid various impediments to effective learning of sacred doctrine, Aquinas is intent to examine all the aspects of the Christian religion in a way that follows the *order of discipline*. The fundamental structure of his theological work reflects Aquinas's authorial intention.

We now begin to follow Aquinas through the form and matter of the *ST* in the *Prima pars*.

The Structure of the *Prima pars* (*ST* I)

Within the *Prima pars*, we can identify three distinct sections. Each of these three sections falls within—and contributes to the unfolding of—the formality of exemplarity.

Prima pars: The Formality of Exemplarity

- Section #1: *ST* I, qq. 2–26: God as one (the divine essence)
- Section #2: *ST* I, qq. 27–43: God as triune (the distinction of Divine Persons—the Trinity)
- Section #3: *ST* I, qq. 44–49: God as creator (the procession of creatures from God)

Aquinas begins in the first section of the *Prima pars* with a consideration of God as one. Specifically, these questions consider the *divine essence*. In the second section, Aquinas examines the *distinction of Divine Persons* in God. Specifically, Aquinas examines the Trinity: God the Father, God the Son, and God the Holy Spirit. Finally, in the third section of the *Prima pars*, Aquinas looks at God as *creator* and the nature of the *creation* he has made.

We note that the progression of the *Prima pars* is a movement from God in himself to God as our creator. This progression is significant both in relation to the formality of exemplarity that unites the *Prima pars* and in relation to the formality of image that follows in the *Secunda pars*. Without a section on the free creation of creatures (and of human persons in particular), there would be no need for the *Secunda pars* or the *Tertia pars* in the *ST*.

Thus, in a very real sense, the *Prima pars* lays the irreplaceable foundation for all that the *ST* considers—from beginning to end. Sacred doctrine is about God chiefly and about all things in reference to God (*ST* I, q. 1). And the *Prima pars* begins with God himself and then accounts for why there are things that are, themselves, *not* God—but must be considered in relation to God.

It is critical to recognize that each of these three parts is fully *about God*. Admittedly, there is a distinction among the *ST*'s considerations of God as one, God as three, and God as creator. The distinction, however, between these considerations does not undermine the fundamental unity of God—God's unity both in himself and as the subject of sacred doctrine. Indeed, this threefold approach to God helps to highlight the unity of God.

God stands at the center of sacred doctrine. And it is to the truth about God himself—as one and as three—that we turn in this chapter.

God's Knowledge of Himself and Our Knowledge of God

Two important details characterize the *ST*'s exposition of the truth about God. First, as we have already noted, the *ST* proceeds in a systematic and scientific manner. This means that the nature and reality of God shapes Aquinas's examination of God.

Second, the *ST* also unfolds according to the requirements of human understanding. Human persons arrive at scientific knowledge through scientific reasoning or discursion. Simply expressed, this means that human persons cannot immediately "see" all truth. We require a step-by-step process in order to understand something. This process applies to all acquired knowledge of the human person in this life. Human persons are creatures. Thus, we cannot understand God in an uncreated way. Human knowledge, by definition, is limited by the type of being that human persons are—beings created in God's image, but truly creatures.

Consequently, we face an interesting paradox: Human persons can come to true knowledge about God. God as he is in himself is truly knowable. Knowledge about God does not water down the truth that is God. Nonetheless, human persons must come to knowledge about God in a human way. This does not insult or compromise his sublimity. Indeed, this bespeaks the dignity of the human person. Human persons *can* come to true knowledge about God—a knowledge that accurately conforms to the truth about him but in an authentically human manner.

God's being and the requirements of human cognition, then, are two principles that Aquinas integrates as he advances through the *ST*'s treatises on God. The truth of divine being is the thread that Aquinas consistently traces throughout the various questions of the *Prima pars*. The order of presentation that Aquinas follows is proportioned to the needs of human understanding.

In short, God's being and knowledge are identical. They are simply God himself. Our being and knowledge, however, are not the same things. We are creatures. We have parts. We understand things through discursive steps and distinctions. Thus, Aquinas's investigation into the truth about God maintains a precise balance between God's simplicity and human complexity.

God as One: The Divine Essence (*ST* I, qq. 2–26)

The first section of the *Prima pars* proceeds in movements. The first movement considers the question, "Does God exist?" (*ST* I, q. 2). The second movement considers how God exists (*ST* I, qq. 3–13). The third movement considers how God operates (*ST* I, qq. 14–26).

The progression of these three questions is both scientific and wise ("sapiential"). Unless we conclude that a given subject actually exists, we cannot hope to have true scientific knowledge about it. After we have determined that the subject of our scientific consideration exists, we must then ask what qualities and attributes characterize the subject. Finally, we must examine how the existing subject acts (or "operates").

*God's Existence (*ST* I, q. 2)*

"The first thing we must know of anything is whether it exists" (*ST* I, q. 2, a. 2, s.c.). In the search for scientific knowledge, the question of existence (in Latin, "*An sit?*") always comes first.

One of the most famous elements of the *ST* appears in *ST* I, q. 2: Aquinas's presentation of his "Five Ways" to discover the existence of God by reason (a. 3). These Five Ways to (sometimes called five "proofs" for) God's existence have intrigued philosophers and theologians for almost eight hundred years.

God's existence is not self-evident—at least, it's not self-evident to us. "Because we do not know the essence of God"—*what* God is—his existence is not self-evident to us. The proposition "God exists," Aquinas explains, "needs to be demonstrated by things that are more known to us . . . namely, by [God's] effects" (a. 1). He explains that while "the existence of truth in general is self-evident" to us, "the existence of a Primal Truth is not self-evident to us" (*ST* I, q. 2, a. 1, ad 3). God is absolutely "primal," that is, first. We are not. Thus, God's existence is self-evident to him, but not to us.

After Aquinas explains why the existence of God is not a truth obvious to the human person, he turns to the question, "Whether it can be demonstrated that God exists?" (*ST* I, q. 2, a. 2). The answer, of course, is yes. God's existence is something that can be demonstrated. Indeed, he justifies his conclusion through reference to Romans 1:20: "The invisible things of Him are clearly seen, being understood by the things that are made." Aquinas explains, "But this would not be unless the existence of God could be demonstrated through the things that are made; for the first thing we must know of anything is whether it exists" (*ST* I, q. 2, a. 2, s.c.). As an instance of divine revelation, Romans 1:20 authoritatively teaches that it is possible to demonstrate God's existence.

It is possible to prove the existence of God "from those of His effects which are known to us" (*ST* I, q. 2, a. 2). Thus, because human reason has access to the effects of God—to the things that God has established in the created order—it is possible to conclude that there is a God. "When an effect is better known to us than its cause, from the effect we proceed to the knowledge of the cause"; indeed, "since every effect depends upon its cause, if the effect exists, the cause must pre-exist" (*ST* I, q. 2, a. 2). And Aquinas's "Five Ways" (*ST* I, q. 2, a. 3) conclude that God exists by reasoning from the effects of God that are evident to human experience and reason.

The fact that God's existence is knowable by reason and that God has revealed his existence through faith points to a significant type of truth: the preambles of the faith (in Latin, *praeambula fidei*). As we saw in chapter 1, philosophy and theology are two distinct sciences. Philosophy rationally proceeds from naturally knowable principles. Sacred doctrine, also, proceeds rationally (*ST* I, q. 1, a. 8). But it proceeds from divinely revealed principles. The vast majority of the articles of the faith are not discoverable by naturally knowable principles. Nonetheless, there are a handful of critically important first truths that are discoverable both by the light of reason and by the light of faith. These are the preambles of the faith (*ST* I, q. 2, a. 2, ad 1). And, what is more, the faith itself teaches that God's existence is discoverable by unaided human reason (*CCC*, 36).

Why are the preambles significant? And why is one of the most important of the preambles of the faith—God's existence—so important?

The demonstrability of God's existence is something that Aquinas (with the Catholic Church) champions because if God were completely inaccessible to human reason, human persons would not be able to receive knowledge of God by faith. The fact that human reason, through its own capacity, can attain some knowledge about God—namely, God's existence and his essential attributes— demonstrates that human reason can receive knowledge from God *beyond* the capacity of reason, namely, through faith. Divine truth is not inimical to human reason—even if divine truth far excels human reason.

These themes classify the examination of God in the *Prima pars* of the *ST* as formally and fully theological. Even if philosophical principles are invoked and human reason is exercised, the *ST* is fully and consistently a work within the ambit of sacred doctrine.

How the One God Exists (ST *I, qq. 3–13)*

"When the existence of a thing has been ascertained there remains the further question of the manner of its existence, in order that we may know its essence" (*ST* I, q. 3, prol.). After examining the demonstrability of God's existence, Aquinas then considers *how* the one God exists. He explores the nature of this existing God through three steps. The first step is through a consideration of how God does not exist (*ST* I, qq. 3–11). The second, how God is known by the human person (*ST* I, q. 12). And finally, he examines how God is named by the human person (*ST* I, q. 13).

How God Is *Not* (*ST* I, qq. 3–11)

Because God transcends the created order—and, subsequently, all created understanding—the most certain way of knowing the truth about God is through discovering what God is *not*. This approach is the only one available to us because we cannot know the divine essence (only God can know adequately and comprehensively the divine essence—to know the divine essence is *to be* the divine essence).

The first topic of discussion is God's simplicity (*ST* I, q. 3). God is not a body nor is he material. Why? Because materiality, by definition, implies limitation. And God, by definition, has no limitations. Indeed, Aquinas shows how God in no way suffers from parts or divisions. He is fully and infinitely one. He is essentially simple. God is simply God.

God does not suffer any of the limitations that are necessarily associated with being composed of parts. Thus, God is pure actuality: No unactualized potential resides in God in any way. He is perfect (*ST* I, q. 4). He lacks nothing. He stands in need of nothing. He acquires nothing.

Were he to lack something and, thus, be able to acquire something, he would not be God. God is pure act. Perfection. There is no unrealized potential in God.

After establishing the fundamental simplicity and perfection of God, Aquinas proceeds to examine the goodness of God (*ST* I, qq. 5–6). "To be good belongs pre-eminently to God" (*ST* I, q. 6, a. 1). Being and goodness are identical in reality. They differ only in created understanding (*ST* I, q. 5, a. 1). God is "the supreme good," absolutely speaking (*ST* I, q. 6, a. 2). He is not a "kind" of good, rather he is goodness itself (*ST* I, q. 6, a. 2). Something is called good in reference to perfection. "God alone has every kind of perfection by His own essence" (*ST* I, q. 6, a. 3). Because he is pure act, his essence and his existence are identical. What does it mean to be God? It simply means to be. To exist. God is existence itself. And, thus, God is—essentially—good. "God alone is good essentially" (*ST* I, q. 6, a. 3). All other beings enjoy goodness in a derivative way, through participating in the divine goodness (*ST* I, q. 6, a. 4).

"After considering the divine perfection," Aquinas explains, "we must consider the divine infinity, and God's existence in things: for God is everywhere, and in all things, inasmuch as He is boundless and infinite" (*ST* I, q. 7, prol.). God is boundless and infinite because he is pure actuality. He is essentially infinite (*ST* I, q. 7, a. 2). There is no principle of limitation or restriction in God. Consequently, God is present to all things as the highest or "first" cause (*ST* I, q. 8, a. 1). Because God's being and his power are identical, God's power, also, suffers no limitations or restriction. He is omnipresent. Everywhere (*ST* I, q. 8, a. 2).

How is God everywhere? He is indeed everywhere, Aquinas explains, by his *power*, *presence*, and *essence* (*ST* I, q. 8, a. 3). All things are subject to his divine power. There is nothing beyond his causal reach. Moreover, all things are present to God—nothing can hide from him or elude his knowledge. Finally, God is present to all things, essentially, as the cause of their being.

Because God is pure act, it is not surprising that he is completely unchangeable or "immutable" (*ST* I, q. 9). Immutability does not mean that God is static as if he were inert. Rather, God is essentially—and exclusively—active. He does not change because there is nothing within him that can change—nothing about him can undergo change or development. Nothing can change God from outside, and nothing within God can undergo change. He is pure perfection.

It is quite common to say that God is eternal, and this is indeed true (*ST* I, q. 10). The reason for God's eternality originates from his pure actuality. God is eternal because he is not subject to time. And he is not subject to time because time is the measurement of change—a dynamic that is completely foreign to God (*ST* I, q. 10, a. 2). There is nothing in God that changes, and therefore there is nothing that time can measure. Time is a succession. Eternity is a simultaneous whole (*ST* I, q. 10, a. 4).

Aquinas concludes this section of the *Prima pars* by emphasizing the fact that God is supremely one. Moreover, there is only one God (*ST* I, q. 11). The student of sacred doctrine is compelled to conclude that there are neither parts nor divisions within God. Moreover, God suffers no outside competition.

How God Is Known by the Human Person (*ST* I, q. 12)

How can human persons know God? Aquinas explains that we can know God through immediate vision (*ST* I, q. 12, aa. 1–11), by reason alone (*ST* I, q. 12, a. 12), and with the help of revelation (*ST* I, q. 12, a. 13).

Because something is knowable insofar as it is actual, God is supremely knowable. He is pure act and, thus, is pure intelligibility.

With regard to the human intellect, however, God is not knowable. Much like the sun before the eyes of an owl, God overwhelms the human mind. As ironic as it might sound, God is *too knowable* for human understanding. Thus, in this life, we cannot see the divine essence.

Nonetheless, God has revealed to us that it is possible for the human mind to see the essence of God. Indeed, this is known as the beatific vision. Heaven. Seeing God face-to-face.

The saints and the angels who enjoy the heavenly vision of God truly see the divine essence. Even so, they do not see God comprehensively (*ST* I, q. 12, a. 7, ad 1). Within the beatific vision, there is no representation of God that is translated into the categories of human knowledge. Even in heaven, God is "too much" for the limitations of human cognition. This causes participants in the beatific vision no chagrin, however. They are fully happy.

The beatific vision requires the *light of glory* (the *lumen gloriae*, in Latin), which serves as a spiritual-intellectual fortification that strengthens the created intellect and enables rational creatures to see the divine essence directly, even if incomprehensively. This light of glory is a created light. It is something *by which* God is seen. We truly see God, but we do not exhaust the essence of God (*ST* I, q. 12, a. 7). Nor do we see everything that is in God (*ST* I, q. 12, a. 8).

In this life, however, no one can see the divine essence, except in the case of a miracle (*ST* I, q. 12, a. 11, ad 2). We can truly know God, however, as our cause, as existing in a way infinitely different from our manner of existence, and as transcending the created order (*ST* I, q. 12, a. 12). Although grace is less potent than the light of glory, grace truly strengthens the natural light of the human intellect (*ST* I, q. 12, a. 13). And through faith we can have certain knowledge about the supernatural mysteries of God, even in this life.

Although the graced light of faith falls short of the light of glory, it is a true light that enables us to know things beyond the native capacity of human reason. It is only in heaven—and under the light of glory—that we can see the divine essence.

How God Is Named by the Human Person (*ST* I, q. 13)

"After the consideration of those things which belong to the divine knowledge, we now proceed to the consideration of the divine names. For everything is named by us according to our knowledge of it" (*ST* I, q. 13, prol.). Question 13 of the *Prima pars*—on the naming of God—may surprise us. Why would Aquinas devote twelve articles to this topic? This question, however, is one of the most important of all those in the *ST*. Why? For the very reason that Aquinas explains: "everything is named by us according to our knowledge of it."

Our understanding is inextricably connected to the human ability to articulate what we understand. And even though we cannot comprehensively "grasp" the divine essence—and must arrive at knowledge about God through what he is not, through a negative way, so to speak—it is nonetheless possible to know, in a piecemeal fashion, truths about God. And because we can arrive at some knowledge about God, it is consequently possible to express the truths that we know about him.

Indeed, we must be able to express what we know. "Naming" something is the culmination of knowledge about something. If we are unable to articulate what we know—even in an inadequate manner—we do not really possess true knowledge.

Hence Aquinas explains that it is possible for human persons to apply words or names to God—like "good" or "wise"—even "substantially." "These names signify the divine substance, and are predicated substantially of God, although they fall short of a full representation of Him" (*ST* I, q. 13, a. 2). Our intellect is able to know truth about God in a creaturely way. Because we are essentially different from God—he is eternal and infinite, we are temporal and finite—we cannot adequately comprehend him. Moreover, our words cannot adequately represent him. But we can point to him as the preeminent principle of all the created perfections and goods that we experience and understand.

"As regards what is signified by these names, they belong properly to God, and more properly than they belong to creatures, and are applied primarily to Him. But as regards their mode of signification, they do not properly and strictly apply to God; for their mode of signification applies to creatures" (*ST* I, q. 13, a. 3). Throughout this question, Aquinas balances the fact that it is possible to articulate the truth about God and yet our words do not adequately reflect the reality of which we speak.

Unsurprisingly, Aquinas emphasizes the fact that God and creatures are essentially different. God is not just "more" than we are. Nor are we simply "less" than God. Rather, we are *essentially different* from God. We are not within the same plane or genus of being. God is in an exclusive "class" of being and existence. And it is here that we find Aquinas's famous theological presentation of *analogy* (*ST* I, q. 13, a. 6).

*How the One God Operates (*ST *I, qq. 14–26)*

In the prologue to *ST* I, q. 14, Aquinas says: "Having considered what belongs to the divine substance, we have now to treat of God's operation." He observes that there are two kinds of operation: "one kind of operation is immanent, and another kind of operation proceeds to the exterior effect, we treat first of knowledge and of will (for understanding abides in the intelligent agent, and will is in the one who wills); and afterwards of the power of God, the principle of the divine operation as proceeding to the exterior effect." Aquinas concludes his consideration of "all that pertains to the unity of the divine essence" with a treatment of "the divine beatitude" (*ST* I, q. 26, prol.).

Thus, we can outline this section of the *Prima pars* in the following manner:

- *ST* I, qq. 14–18: God's knowledge
- *ST* I, qq. 19–24: God's will
- *ST* I, qq. 25–26: God's power and beatitude

God's Knowledge (*ST* I, qq. 14–18)

In light of God's infinite perfection, it is unsurprising that Aquinas maintains that in God there is most perfect knowledge. Indeed, God's knowledge is his substance, and his substance is pure actuality. Thus, God understands himself *through himself*—and he alone comprehends himself perfectly.

Of course, God also knows things other than himself. In fact, God knows other things in and through his own divine essence. Here, Aquinas emphasizes that God knows the exemplar formality of the things that he has created (*ST* I, q. 14, a. 5). Consequently, he knows things other than himself, not merely generically, but in a proper and specific way.

Unlike our knowledge, God sees all things at once and in reference to himself—as the supreme cause of all effects (*ST* I, q. 14, a. 7). God knows everything that he brings into being and existence at any time ("knowledge of approbation"). He also knows everything that ever was and ever will be ("knowledge of vision"). Finally, in God's "simple understanding," he also knows things that do not, did not, and never will exist (*ST* I, q. 14, a. 9).

In sum, nothing is outside of God's knowledge, and his knowledge is shaped by nothing other than himself. Truth is the conformity of the mind with reality (*ST* I, q. 16, a. 2). Thus, God is, quite literally, truth itself—his being and knowledge are identical and account for all that is (*ST* I, q. 16, a. 5). God is infinitely living and vital (*ST* I, q. 18).

God's Will (*ST* I, qq. 19–24)

Because the dynamics of willing necessarily follows upon the dynamics of knowing, God also has a will. And as God is his intellect, so too is God his will.

The activating object of the intellect is being. The activating object of the will is the good. We will something in order to attain something.

God, however, lacks nothing. Therefore, God's will and God's love only delight in what he possesses. Hence, the divine essence itself is the object of the divine will. And without any exaggeration, Aquinas concludes that God wills himself (*ST* I, q. 19). God wills himself in the sense that he delights in his own existence—not in the sense that he wills himself into being.

God also wills creatures and things other than himself. Hence, he wills other things in reference to himself as the end of all other things that he has created (*ST* I, q. 19, a. 2). Nothing outside of God causes God to will something (*ST* I, q. 19, a. 5). Nor is God's will in any way frustrated (*ST* I, q. 19, a. 6). As God's being undergoes no development, so God's will undergoes no change. Nonetheless, God can will change in other things. But when God wills, he does not impose necessity on the things that he wills (*ST* I, q. 19, a. 8). Aquinas says that God wills necessary things necessarily and contingent things contingently. The profundity of God's causality is such that he not only wills *that* certain things occur but also the manner or the mode that they occur. In other words, God wills both *what* happens and *how* things happen.

Because God is supremely good, God does not will sin and moral evil (*ST* I, q. 19, a. 9). The object of the will is always the good. Evil is never intended in itself but only in relation to some other disordered good. Nonetheless, God does permit some evils to occur (*ST* I, q. 19, a. 9, ad 3). And he always brings about a greater good through them.

Because God wills nothing outside of himself under any compulsion, God's will is undetermined by any created thing. He is free with regard to all that he creates and governs. And love (*ST* I, q. 20), justice, and mercy (*ST* I, q. 21) all "absolutely pertain to the divine will" (*ST* I, q. 20, prol.).

Finally, Aquinas expounds upon those things that pertain both to the divine intellect and to the divine will, namely, providence, predestination, and the book of life. He explains that providence refers to God's knowledge of "all created things," while predestination is a subset of providence and pertains to the human person specifically: "man as regards his eternal salvation" (*ST* I, q. 22, prol.). The book of life metaphorically refers to God's knowledge of the predestined—and most especially of those predestined to glory (and not only to grace) (*ST* I, q. 24). Because of his complete knowledge of all created things, God knows who will be saved.

God's Power and Beatitude (*ST* I, qq. 25–26)

In *ST* I, q. 25, Aquinas considers the divine power. As we have already seen, God is pure actuality. Thus, he is omnipotent. He can do all possible things. "God is bound to nobody but Himself. Hence, when it is said that God can only do what He ought, nothing else is meant by this than that God can do nothing but what is befitting to Himself, and just" (*ST* I, q. 25, a. 5, ad 2). God cannot, however, perform things that are intrinsically contradictory. With regard to contradictory things, Aquinas says that "it is better to say that such things cannot be done, than that God cannot do them" (*ST* I, q. 25, a. 3).

Aquinas concludes his examination of "all that pertains to the unity of the divine essence" by considering divine beatitude (*ST* I, q. 26, prol.). He explains that "beatitude belongs to God in a very special manner." Beatitude is "the perfect good of an intellectual nature; which is capable of knowing that it has a sufficiency of the good which it possesses, to which it is competent that good or ill may befall, and which can control its own actions." All of these qualifications of beatitude apply to God in a preeminent way: "Whence beatitude belongs to God in the highest degree" (*ST* I, q. 26, a. 1).

God as Triune: The Distinction of Divine Persons (*ST* I, qq. 27–43)

"Having considered what belongs to the unity of the divine essence, it remains to treat of what belongs to the Trinity of the persons in God" (*ST* I, q. 27, prol.). This section proceeds in three movements:

- *ST* I, q. 27: The origin or procession of the Divine Persons
- *ST* I, q. 28: The relations of origin
- *ST* I, qq. 29–43: The Divine Persons

*The Origin or Procession of Divine Persons (*ST *I, q. 27)*

Aquinas highlights the fact that the Bible explicitly references the procession or "origin" of Trinitarian Persons. Indeed, "Divine Scripture uses, in relation to God, names which signify procession" (*ST* I, q. 27,

a. 1). Something can "proceed" in different ways, however. Aquinas is exceedingly careful to clarify the precise meaning of procession in God.

He explains that the procession of the Son from the Father and the procession of the Holy Spirit from the Father and the Son cannot mean "an outward act" (*ST* I, q. 27, a. 1). Trinitarian procession is *immanent*—interior or inward action. There are two such processions in God: the eternal procession of the Word by "intelligible action," and the eternal procession of Love by way of the divine will (*ST* I, q. 27, a. 3). These are both immanent processions. Thus, in the case of the Word's procession, the known is in the knower. And in the case of Love's procession, the beloved is in the lover.

The procession of the Word in God is called *generation*. And the Word as proceeding in God is called the Son (*ST* I, q. 27, a. 2). The Son eternally receives his existence from the Eternal Father—he eternally receives the entirety of the divine nature from the Father (*ST* I, q. 27, a. 2, ad 3). The Word is eternally conceived by the Father, and the Word has the same divine nature as the Father.

The procession of the Love in God is as *spiration*—"as it is a procession of the [Holy] Spirit" (*ST* I, q. 27, a. 4, ad 3). "Spiration" signifies "a certain vital movement and impulse, accordingly as anyone is described as moved or impelled by love to perform an action" (*ST* I, q. 27, a. 4).

These are the only two processions within God. Aquinas reminds us that "God understands all things by one simple act; and by one act also He wills all things. Hence there cannot exist in Him a procession of Word from Word, nor of Love from Love: for there is in Him only one perfect Word, and one perfect Love; thereby being manifested His perfect fecundity" (*ST* I, q. 27, a. 5).

The Relations of Origin (ST I, q. 28)

The real processions in God reveal that there are also real relations in God. "In respect of each of these processions two opposite relations arise; one of which is the relation of the person proceeding from the principle; the other is the relation of the principle Himself" (*ST* I, q. 28, a. 4).

Specifically, Aquinas explains that there are only four real relations in God: paternity, filiation, spiration, and procession (*ST* I, q. 28, a. 4). As we have seen, the Son's generation is procession by way of intellect. Thus, the relation of the principle to the generated is called *paternity*, and the relation of the generated to the principle of generation is called *filiation*. In the Holy Spirit's procession, the relation of the principle to the spirated is known as *spiration*, and the relation of the spirated to the principle is known as *procession*.

The Divine Persons (ST I, qq. 29–43)

With regard to the Divine Persons of the Trinity, Aquinas first considers the nature of divine personhood in general (*ST* I, qq. 29–32) and then considers the Divine Persons in particular (*ST* I, qq. 33–38). In the general consideration, he examines Boethius's famous definition of "person": "an individual substance of a rational nature" (*ST* I, q. 29). A "person" refers to a thing that exists in itself and not in another. The three Divine Persons share the same divine nature, and therefore "person" in the Trinity refers not to three individual natures but to three *subsisting relations*: "'person' signifies in God a relation as subsisting in the divine nature" (*ST* I, q. 30, a. 1).

Aquinas then considers the number of the Divine Persons: Father, Son, and Holy Spirit (*ST* I, q. 30). The Father is subsisting paternity, the Son is subsisting filiation, and the Holy Spirit is subsisting procession (*ST* I, q. 30, a. 2). These are the three subsisting relations in God. Consequently, "the name 'Trinity' in God signifies the determinate number of persons" (*ST* I, q. 31, a. 1).

Finally, Aquinas concludes his general overview of the Trinitarian persons by considering how we can know the Divine Persons (*ST* I, q. 32). He explains that we cannot discover the triunity of God by reason alone. Faith is the only way we can discover that the One God is Three in Person (*ST* I, q. 32, a. 1). Additionally, there are *notions* in God. Aquinas explains that "a notion is the proper idea whereby we know a divine Person" (*ST* I, q. 32, a. 3). There are five notions in God: innascibility (the unbegottenness of the Father), paternity, filiation, common spiration, and procession.

In *ST* I, qq. 33–38, Aquinas considers the Divine Persons in particular, specifically considering the person and proper names of the Father, of the Son, and of the Holy Spirit. After "those things considered which belong to the divine persons absolutely," Aquinas explains that "we next treat of what concerns the person in reference to the essence [*ST* I, q. 39], to the properties [*ST* I, q. 40], and to the notional acts [*ST* I, q. 41]." He then concludes the *ST*'s study of the Holy Trinity with a "comparison of these with each other [*ST* I, qq. 42–43]" (*ST* I, q. 39, prol.).

Throughout these remaining questions, Aquinas continues to exposit the unity and the distinction between God as one and God as three. He devotes special attention to the way that human understanding and language about God as one and God as three is both limited and yet can accurately reflect and express the truth about God in himself. Indeed, these themes consistently characterize Aquinas's entire presentation of God—the subject of sacred doctrine.

Chapter Six

God as Creator

(ST I, qq. 44–119)

In the prologue to *ST* I, q. 44, Aquinas turns his attention to "the procession of creatures from God." This consideration of creaturely procession, of course, suitably follows his consideration of the procession of the Divine Persons within God. Aquinas explains that his examination of the nature and dynamics of creation comprises three sections:

- Section 1: *ST* I, qq. 44–46: The production of creatures
- Section 2: *ST* I, qq. 47–102: The distinction between creatures
- Section 3: *ST* I, qq. 103–119: The preservation and government of creatures

As we noted in the previous chapter, the progression of the *Prima pars* from God in himself to God as our creator is of critical importance for the structure of the *ST*.

Exemplarity is the formality that integrates and directs the *Prima pars*. The *ST*'s extensive consideration of God as creator is essential to this formality. Exemplarity is a relative notion. An exemplar requires something that is "exemplated," or made according to the pattern of the divine exemplar ideas. Every being that God creates reflects God's ideas about created reality. Thus, the formality of exemplarity only applies to the *Prima pars* because the *ST* considers God as creator in addition to God as one and three.

Therefore, the *ST*'s examination of God as creator and of the nature of creation is essential to Aquinas's order of discipline and the presentation of sacred doctrine.

The Production of Creatures (*ST* I, qq. 44–46)

ST I, q. 44 contains, in summary form, the fundamental principles of the *ST*'s presentation of creation. Here, Aquinas examines whether the procession of creatures from God proceeds according to the four causes: efficient, material, formal, and final. Taking the example of a chair, there are four things that cause it to be what it is: the carpenter who built it (the efficient cause), the wood used to construct it (the material cause), the design of its shape in the mind of the carpenter and in the chair itself (the formal cause), and its ultimate purpose of providing a place to sit (the final cause).

ST I, q. 44, a. 1 considers whether it is necessary that every being be created by God. The conclusion is clear: "Every being in any way existing is from God" (*ST* I, q. 44, a. 1). This article considers efficient causality—namely, God as the agent who directly and immediately produces what he creates. The conclusion advanced in this article follows upon the nature of God as well as the nature of contingent being. God is simple. He is self-subsistent being. He has no explanation for his being outside of himself. Therefore, Aquinas says, all beings other than God are not their own being. Rather, they are beings by participation.

Aquinas also demonstrates that even the material foundations for composite being fall within the ambit of divine causality. God is the cause of materiality even if materiality is never found in a state of pure materiality (i.e., "prime" or "primary matter"—matter without any formal principle).

With regard to formal causality, Aquinas reiterates one of the key themes of the *Prima pars*: that God is the first exemplar cause of all things. God possesses the knowledge of what he creates. Creation bears these divine ideas in the very structures of created reality.

Finally, in *ST* q. 44, a. 4, Aquinas argues that God is the final cause, the *end*, of all things. He explains that every agent (i.e., a being that acts or causes) acts for an end. Unlike creatures, however, God does not act in order to obtain some type of perfection or goodness. He is pure act. He suffers no privations of goodness. Rather, he acts outside of himself to share his goodness and perfection. Thus, the divine goodness is the end of all things. God does not act for "His own profit" but only on account of his own goodness (*ST* I, q. 44, a. 4, ad 1). Consequently, all things desire God as their end because all good things reflect and are ordered to the divine goodness (*ST* I, q. 44, a. 4, ad 3).

Aquinas concludes *ST* I, q. 44 with a precise summary of the conclusions that punctuate the remainder of the *Prima pars*: "Since God is the efficient, the exemplar and the final cause of all things, and since primary matter is from Him, it follows that the first principle of all things is one in reality" (*ST* I, q. 44, a. 4, ad 4).

*Creation: "From Nothing" (*Ex Nihilo*)*

ST I, q. 45 "concerns the mode of the emanation of things from the First Principle, and this is called creation" (*ST* I, q. 45, prol.). God is the First Principle from whom all things proceed. Aquinas thus considers the way that creatures proceed from God.

Building upon *ST* I, q. 44, Aquinas explains that it is not only necessary to consider the "emanation of a particular thing" from some particular agent. The theologian must also consider "the emanation of all being from a universal cause, which is God" (*ST* I, q. 45, a. 1). This emanation of all being from God is *creation*. In other words, creation does not refer to mere "generation" or "alteration." Why? Such types of changes presuppose a prior existing thing that is generated or altered. Creation, in contrast, refers to the coming into being of "the whole substance" of a thing. And this type of complete coming into being arises from utter "not-being" (*ST* I, q. 45, a. 1, ad 2).

God creates "from nothing" (*ex nihilo*, in Latin). Aquinas explains that the preposition "from" does not mean that God creates something "out of nothing" in the (ridiculous) sense that God uses nothing to create something—as if "nothing" were a kind of raw material principle. Rather, when we say that God creates "from nothing" we are speaking of *order*: Creation comes "from" nothing in the sense that it comes *after* nothing: "As when we say, 'from morning comes midday'—i.e., after morning is midday" (*ST* I, q. 45, a. 1, ad 3).

"It is necessary to say that all things were created by God" (*ST* I, q. 45, a. 2). God alone can create (*ST* I, q. 45, a. 5). Other beings can introduce change into things that already exist (*ST* I, q. 45, a. 2, ad 2), but only God can create because only God can create from nothing. Moreover, "to create is not proper to any one [Trinitarian] Person, but is common to the whole Trinity" (*ST* I, q. 45, a. 6). "Nevertheless," Aquinas observes, "the divine Persons, according to the nature of their procession, have a causality respecting the creation of things"—the processions are the "type of the productions of creatures" (*ST* I, q. 45, a. 6).

In creation, God produces a thing without any change or motion (because there is nothing prior to creation). Thus, the only thing that remains—in the absence of change or motion—is a relation in the creature. "Creation in the creature is only a certain relation to the Creator as to the principle of its being" (*ST* I, q. 45, a. 3).

*The Beginning of the Duration of Creatures (*ST* I, q. 46)*

In *ST* I, q. 46, Aquinas considers whether it is possible that creatures always existed. Because "it is not necessary that God will anything except himself," it follows that "it is not necessary for God to will that the world should always exist" (*ST* I, q. 46, a. 1). The fact that God was not obligated to create—and that he freely chose to create—renders it impossible to prove demonstratively that the world always existed. Moreover, "by faith alone do we hold, and by no demonstration can it be proved, that the world did not always exist" (*ST* I, q. 46, a. 2). Only God's revelation can manifest the free decision of the divine will; thus, the fact that the universe had a beginning is something that we cannot discover by reason alone.

Genesis 1:1 plays an important role in the *ST*'s presentation of the duration of creation: "In the beginning God created heaven and earth." Aquinas clarifies that "things are said to be created in the beginning of time, not as if the beginning of time were a measure of creation, but because together with time heaven and earth were created" (*ST* I, q. 46, a. 3, ad 1).

The Distinction Between Creatures (*ST* I, qq. 47–102)

"After considering the production of creatures, we come to the consideration of the distinction of things" (*ST* I, q. 47, prol.). This consideration comprises three parts:

- *ST* I, q. 47: The distinction of things in general
- *ST* I, qq. 48–49: The distinction of good and evil
- *ST* I, qq. 50–101: The distinction of the spiritual and corporeal creature

Although all created things share the same origin—God created them from nothing—there is great variety among them. Essential and accidental (or qualitative) differences characterize the things that God has created. In other words, there are things that do not have the same nature (e.g., a tree and a trout are essentially different), and there are things that have the same nature but are still accidentally different (e.g., two puppies of different breeds).

"The distinction and multitude of things come from the intention of the first agent, who is God" (*ST* I, q. 47, a. 1). God "brought things into being in order that His goodness might be communicated to creatures, and be represented by them." By definition, however, no created thing can "adequately represent" the divine goodness. A creature is necessarily and intrinsically limited. Thus, it is impossible for any creature to reflect, comprehensively, the infinite goodness of God. "Goodness, which in God is simple and uniform, in creatures is manifold and divided and hence the whole universe together participates the divine goodness more perfectly, and represents it better than any single creature whatever" (*ST* I, q. 47, a. 1).

God wisely created different things to exist differently. Moreover, God's wisdom also explains why created things are not equal. There is a hierarchy in creation. "For the universe would not be perfect if only one grade of goodness were found in things" (*ST* I, q. 47, a. 2). The perfection of the universe requires that there be degrees of goodness in different created things.

The Distinction Between Good and Evil (ST *I, qq. 48–49)*

After examining the distinction between created things in general, Aquinas proceeds to consider the distinction between things in particular. He identifies two particular distinctions: (1) the distinction between good and evil (*ST* I, qq. 48–49), and (2) the distinction between purely spiritual creatures and bodily creatures (*ST* I, qq. 50–101).

Aquinas explains the distinction between good and evil by reminding his readers that "evil" means "the absence of good" (*ST* I, q. 48, a. 1). Evil is not so much a "something" as it is the deprivation of something—or, in other words, the absence of due goodness. Thus, evil is parasitic. There can be pure goodness, but there cannot exist anything that is "purely evil." Nor is there "one supreme evil" that is the cause of every evil (*ST* I, q. 49, a. 3). Thus, "as darkness is known through light," so "what evil is must be known from the nature of good." Aquinas concludes: "Hence it cannot be that evil signifies being, or any form or nature" (*ST* I, q. 48, a. 1).

Thus, evil is a *privation* or an absence of a due good in an existing thing (*ST* I, q. 41, a. 2, ad 1). Evil truly exists, but it exists in something that is ordered to the good—to a perfective end. "Now it is in this that evil consists, namely, in the fact that a thing fails in goodness. Hence it is clear that evil is found in things, as corruption also is found; for corruption is itself an evil" (*ST* I, q. 48, a. 2).

Aquinas continues to clarify that "not every absence of good is evil" (*ST* I, q. 48, a. 3). For example, the fact that a rock cannot see is not a physical evil. Why? The nature of a rock is not ordered to sight. The rock suffers no privation of a due good by its lack of sight. In contrast, the human eye is ordered to sight. Thus, we would describe blindness in the human eye as a physical evil—the absence of a due good.

Because evil is parasitic, "evil cannot wholly consume the good" (*ST* I, q. 48, a. 4). Evil does not subsist—it is a privation in something that is good—and therefore evil cannot deprive a being of the fundamental goodness of that being's existence. Nonetheless, "there is also a kind of good which is diminished by evil, but is not wholly taken away; and this good is the aptitude of a subject to some actuality" (*ST* I, q. 48, a. 4). Evil frustrates a being's fundamental orientation to perfective goodness. Thus, evil cannot destroy goodness entirely but does contravene the actualization of goodness in a being.

Aquinas also explains there are *two kinds of evil* that follow upon a being's twofold orientation to goodness: "Evil, as was said above, is the privation of good, which chiefly and of itself consists in perfection and act. Act, however, is twofold; first, and second" (*ST* I, q. 48, a. 5). "First act is the form and integrity of a thing," the fundamental goodness of its being, while "second act is its operation," the actions that a thing performs in order to achieve its fulfillment (*ST* I, q. 48, a. 5).

Therefore, one type of evil contradicts the goodness of first act, and the other type of evil frustrates the goodness of second act. The first type of evil is called the "evil of pain" (or "punishment" or "penalty"—*poena*, in Latin). An example of the evil of pain is blindness, for blindness is a type of "withdrawal of the form and integrity" of a thing (in this case, an eye). The second type of evil is called the "evil of fault" (or "guilt").

This second type of evil is properly *moral evil*—the evil of freely chosen operations or actions.

Aquinas explains that "fault has the nature of evil more than pain has" (*ST* I, q. 48, a. 6). "One becomes evil by the evil of fault, but not by the evil of pain . . . since good absolutely considered consists in act, and not in potentiality." Moral evil is far more evil than mere pain: "Because the fault itself consists in the disordered act of the will, and the pain consists in the privation of something used by the will, fault has more of evil in it than pain has" (*ST* I, q. 48, a. 6). The evil of pain can take away a created good (e.g., blindness deprives the eye of sight), but the evil of fault (i.e., moral evil) is opposed to uncreated goodness. The evil of fault is objectively "opposed to the fulfillment of the divine will, and to divine love" (*ST* I, q. 48, a. 6).

Aquinas concludes, "therefore, every evil in voluntary things is to be looked upon as a pain or a fault" (*ST* I, q. 48, a. 5). The evil of fault is always voluntary. In contrast, the evil of pain is against the fundamental orientation of the will.

Moreover, it is evident that "God is the author of the evil of pain, but not of the evil of fault" (*ST* I, q. 48, a. 6). God establishes things in goodness. "God, by causing in things the good of the order of the universe, consequently and as it were by accident, causes the corruptions of things" (*ST* I, q. 49, a. 2). God is not in any way, however, the cause of the evil of fault.

The Distinction Between Spiritual and Bodily Creatures (ST I, qq. 50–102)

After Aquinas explains the distinction between good and evil (and the distinction between the two types of evil), he then considers "the distinction of corporeal and spiritual creatures: firstly, the purely spiritual creature which in Holy Scripture is called angel; secondly, the creature wholly corporeal; thirdly, the composite creature, corporeal and spiritual, which is man" (*ST* I, q. 50, prol.).

- The angels—purely spiritual creatures—are considered first (*ST* I, qq. 50–64).
- Purely corporeal creatures—the six days of creation—are considered second (*ST* I, qq. 65–74).

- Finally, the human person—as a united composite of spirit (soul) and body (corporeity)—comes third (*ST* I, qq. 75–102).

The order of these three treatises is noteworthy. Aquinas begins with the angels because they are the naturally highest of all creatures. The nature and operations of the angels are vastly superior to all other created natures and natural modes of operation. The treatise on the human person falls after the treatise on the angels as well as the treatise on corporeal creatures because humans comprise both spiritual and material principles. The human person is an essentially different kind of being from the angels and from corporeal creatures. Nonetheless, the human person is a kind of "microcosmos," uniquely participating in the spiritual and the material orders of the universe God has created.

The Angels (*ST* I, qq. 50–64)

The angels are purely spiritual beings; they are not composed of matter and form (*ST* I, q. 50, a. 2). They are "altogether incorporeal" (*ST* I, q. 50, a. 1). Aquinas explains that their being and existence are necessary because of the intention of God as creator: "For what is principally intended by God in creatures is good, and this consists in assimilation to God Himself." And because God creates "by his intellect and will . . . the perfection of the universe requires that there should be intellectual creatures"—spiritual creatures (*ST* I, q. 50, a. 1). The angels "rank between God and the corporeal creatures" (*ST* I, q. 50, a. 1, ad 1).

As the naturally highest of all creatures, the angels exist "in exceeding great number, far beyond all material multitude." Why? "Because, since it is the perfection of the universe that God chiefly intends in the creation of things, the more perfect some things are, in so much greater an excess are they created by God" (*ST* I, q. 50, a. 3). The perfection of the universe requires that such sublime beings exist in a vast quantity.

The real creatureliness of the angels is an important theme in the *ST*. God alone is infinite and pure act. "Although there is no composition of matter and form in an angel, yet there is act and potentiality" (*ST* I, q. 50, a. 2, ad 3). The angels are pure forms, but they are still forms whose essence is really distinct from their existence. Because corruption (or death) is the separation of form from matter, angels do not deteriorate or die. They do not have bodies—although they can assume bodily appearance for the sake of their mission (*ST* I, q. 51). They are incorruptible

(*ST* I, q. 50, a. 5). Moreover, given their purely formal nature (i.e., being completely immaterial), each angel is radically unique (*ST* I, q. 50, a. 4).

Because the angels do not have bodies, they cannot be said "to be contained by a place" (*ST* I, q. 52, a. 1). Rather, "the angel is in a place by the application of his power to the place." Thus, an angel is present to someone or something through the exercise of causality on someone or something. And, because an angel is a creature, "he is not everywhere, nor in several places, but in only one place" at a given time (*ST* I, 52, a. 2). An angel is said to "move locally" or to "change places" insofar as "he can all at once quit the whole place, and in the same instant apply himself to the whole of another place" (*ST* I, q. 53, a. 1).

As we have already seen, angels know and love (*ST* I, q. 59, a. 1). Unlike God, however, angelic being is not identical with the act of angelic knowledge and love (*ST* I, q. 54). Angels do not know everything by way of their essence (*ST* I, q. 55, a. 1). Rather, "they received from God the species of things known, together with their intellectual nature" (*ST* I, q. 55, a. 2). God imparts to them the concepts through which they know reality. What angels know, however, is simpler and more comprehensive than our human knowledge: "in the truths which they know naturally, they at once behold all things whatsoever that can be known in them" (*ST* I, q. 58, a. 3). Moreover, angelic love bears the sublime characteristics of angelic knowledge (*ST* I, q. 60).

The Six Days of Creation (*ST* I, qq. 65–74)

Aquinas's consideration of corporeal creatures focuses upon the account of creation found in Genesis 1. He explains that the production of corporeal creatures, recounted in the beginning of the Bible, comprises "three works": the "work of creation," the "work of distinction," and the "work of adornment" (*ST* I, q. 65, prol.). In Aquinas's presentation of each of these three works, he integrates the following elements: the biblical account of creation, the relevant philosophical principles, and the accounts of creation found in the church fathers and in significant theologians.

Aquinas's presentation of the work of creation emphasizes that God alone is the creator (*ST* I, q. 65). With regard to the work of distinction, Aquinas first explains the dynamics of form and matter with regard to the creation of the heavens and of the earth (*ST* I, q. 67). He then examines the key distinctions found in the first three days of creation:

light, darkness, firmament, waters, and plants (*ST* I, qq. 67–69). Finally, in Aquinas's presentation of the work of adornment, he homes in on the themes present in the fourth through sixth days of creation: light, sky animals, water animals, and land animals (*ST* I, qq. 70–72). The final questions of this treatise consider the seventh day and the completion of creation (*ST* I, q. 73) as well as the seven days in common (*ST* I, q. 74).

The Human Person (*ST* I, qq. 75–102)

Aquinas divides his examination of the human person into two main sections: "the nature of man" and "his origin" (*ST* I, q. 75, prol.). He clarifies that "the theologian considers the nature of man in relation to the soul; but not in relation to the body, except in so far as the body has relation to the soul" (*ST* I, q. 75, prol.). Thus, the soul is of paramount significance in this treatise of the *ST*.

Nonetheless, Aquinas consistently emphasizes that the human person is not only a soul but rather a union of soul and body (*ST* I, q. 76). The human soul is not a mere "motor" trapped within a body (*ST* I, q. 76, a. 8); instead, the human "intellectual soul is united to the body as the substantial form" (*ST* I, q. 76, a. 6). The rational soul is the principle of the life of the body. During human life, "the soul must be in the whole body, and in each part thereof" (*ST* I, q. 76, a. 8).

Aquinas explains that the concerns of the theologian extend to the "intellectual and appetitive powers" of the soul, "in which the virtues reside" (*ST* I, q. 78, prol.). The intellect is ordered to being; appetite is ordered to goodness.

He emphasizes that all of human knowledge arises from contact with the external world through the five senses (*ST* I, q. 78). Human sensation gives rise to sense knowledge in the human person. The human intellect is able to receive and process the sense data received through sense experience and arrive at a knowledge of "universal being" (*ST* I, q. 79, a. 2). This means that the intellect can grasp the nature of things in an immaterial way—in a mode consonant with the immaterial nature of the human intellect itself (*ST* I, q. 79). Throughout Aquinas's presentation of the dynamics of the human intellect, he is emphatic that the human person can really know the truth about reality, even if the process requires an elaborate path of discovery and reasoning.

Every being has a *natural appetite* for goodness, a fundamental inclination of a being to its proper good (*ST* I, q. 80, a. 1). With regard to the appetitive powers of the soul (those powers that seek the good and different kinds of goodness), Aquinas explains that the human person has two really distinct types of appetite—sensitive and intellectual—arising from the different types of knowledge (*ST* I, q. 80, a. 2). The sensitive (or sense) appetite is activated by sensible goods. The intellectual (or rational) appetite is activated by intellectually known goodness—that is, "universal goodness," or something good in any way.

Sense knowledge is always about individuals and particulars. Thus, the sense appetites are only activated by individual and particular goods (e.g., a good steak or drink). The sense appetites cannot desire a good that is immaterial. In contrast, the rational appetite can be activated by *any* good—whether individual and particular or spiritual and immaterial. The will's proper object is universal goodness—goodness itself.

The will's essential orientation to universal goodness explains why the will is free. Although the will necessarily only wills good things, the will does not necessarily will any particular good thing. "The will can tend to nothing except under the aspect of good. But because good is of many kinds, for this reason the will is not of necessity determined to one" (*ST* I, q. 82, a. 2, ad 1). Only when the intellect sees God face-to-face in the beatific vision—and sees immediately the one being who is good in every respect—will the will not be free. "The will of the man who sees God in His essence of necessity adheres to God, just as now we desire of necessity to be happy" (*ST* I, q. 82, a. 2).

Of course, Aquinas considers many other topics in his treatise on the human person. He devotes attention to how the human intellect knows different types of things in this life (*ST* I, qq. 85–88) and after death (*ST* I, q. 89). Moreover, he devotes numerous questions to the "first production of man: (1) the production of man himself; (2) the end of this production; (3) the state and the condition of the first man; the place of his abode" (*ST* I, q. 90, prol.). Aquinas clearly explains that the first humans were created in a state of grace and possessed virtue (*ST* I, q. 95). He concludes by describing the unique spiritual and bodily privileges that the first humans enjoyed in their pre-Fall state of innocence (*ST* I, qq. 96–102).

The Preservation and Government of Creatures (*ST* I, qq. 103–119)

Aquinas concludes the *Prima pars* by examining how God *governs* and directs his creatures. Aquinas expresses the essential theme of this treatise most succinctly: "It belongs to the Divine goodness, as it brought things into existence, so to lead them to their end: and this is to govern" (*ST* I, q. 103, a. 1). As God gives existence to the things that he creates (and sustains them in existence), so does he order them to their perfective ends (*ST* I, q. 103, a. 5). No creature falls outside of the ordering of divine goodness. God is the beginning and the end of all created things (*ST* I, q. 103, a. 2).

Consequently, God's causality extends to all beings in all their respective dimensions (*ST* I, q. 105). Thus, the power of divine causality touches on all created principles—God sustains all things in being, and he can move all things from within: the body, the intellect, and even the will. No part of created reality is outside God's governing direction.

Of course, God has ordered the created universe such that other creatures can also participate—as subordinate causes—in the fulfillment of his wisdom and love. The angels, specifically, play significant roles in the "movement" of other creatures (*ST* I, qq. 106–114). Nonetheless, other creatures—corporeal creatures and human persons—also participate in the order of the universe as real secondary causes.

The closing sections of the *ST*'s *Prima pars* amount to a profound reflection on the fact that God is absolutely first and supreme in the order of things. Nothing is above God. Nothing is beyond God. God is causally present to all things in all their respective parts and dimensions.

And yet God's wisdom and power do not denigrate the creatures he governs. Quite the contrary: There is no competitive tension between God and the creature. Indeed, given the nature of God and the nature of the creature, any such competition would be impossible.

In his wisdom, God orders all things so profoundly, powerfully, and sweetly that his creatures share in the order of the universe as true and dignified causes. Because of God, each creature has its own part in the universe—and each creature fully plays its part.

I-II. The First Part of the Second Part: Christian Moral Principles

CHAPTER 7

God: The End of the Human Person

(ST I-II, qq. 1–5)

As we saw in chapter 4, the *ST* is structured around the dynamics of exemplarity and the human person as created in the image of God (*ad imaginem Dei*). This structure explains why Aquinas begins his consideration of the Christian life as follows: "In this matter we shall consider first the last end of human life; and secondly, those things by means of which man may advance towards his end, or stray from the path: for the end is the rule of whatever is ordained to the end" (*ST* I-II, q. 1, prol.). The prologue to the first question of the *Prima secundae* clarifies the unity between what Aquinas considers in the *Prima pars* with what follows in the *Secunda pars*.

We recall from chapter 3 that God has revealed sacred doctrine because God himself is the supernatural end of the human person. Therefore, there is an intrinsically salvific nature and purpose to sacred doctrine itself. In the *Prima pars*, the *ST* began with God in himself and progressed to what God does outside himself (i.e., creation and governance). The *Secunda pars* examines the human person's advancement toward God by knowledge and love. And this second part of the *ST* is intelligible only because of who God is in himself (i.e., the supreme good) and the fact that God freely chose to create.

The human person can advance toward God by knowledge and love only because human nature was created in the image of God. Human nature, in turn, was created in the image of God because God freely chose to create human persons according to his knowledge of—and love for—himself. All of this helps to explain why Aquinas begins the second part of the *ST* with a consideration of God as "man's last end." God is the center of both the exemplarity formality of the *Prima pars* and the image formality of the *Secunda pars*.

Aquinas devotes the first five questions of the *Prima secundae* to man's last end. He explains that the five questions can be divided into the following two broad groupings:

- Man's last end in general (*ST* I-II, q. 1)
- Man's last end in particular—happiness (or "beatitude") (*ST* I-II, qq. 2–5)

These five questions set up the parameters for all that Aquinas considers in the remainder of the *Secunda pars* (in both the *Prima secundae* and the *Secunda secundae*).

The *Secunda pars* is the largest part of the *ST*. In the prologue to the *Secunda secundae*, Aquinas explains the distinction between the *Prima secundae* and the *Secunda secundae*: "After a general consideration of virtues, vices, and other things pertaining to moral matters, it is necessary to consider each of them in particular" (*ST* II-II, prol.). Thus, the *Prima secundae* examines the general principles of Christian morality. The *Secunda secundae* examines in a particular and individual way the various virtues and opposing vices that characterize Christian morality. Here, again, Aquinas's order of discipline assumes a wise, sapiential structure. Aquinas begins with universal principles and then advances to more concrete implications and applications of the universal principles.

Man's Last End in General (*ST* I-II, q. 1)

Aquinas commences his presentation of the general principles of Christian morality with the question: "What is the ultimate end of the human person?" In other words, Aquinas starts with the final cause of the Christian life. The answer that emerges throughout the course of his rigorous analysis is consonant with the themes that run throughout the *Prima pars*: God is the end of the human person.

It is impossible to overexaggerate the importance of the end in any reflection on reality. Every nature is ordered to an end, and every being acts for the sake of an end. An "end-less being" is both impossible and unintelligible. Everything exists with a purpose. And everything is understood in reference to this purpose. Thus, finality shapes all of reality—and all knowledge of reality.

Aquinas explains that "it belongs to man to do everything for an end" (*ST* I-II, q. 1, s.c.). He proceeds to explain that an action is *human* insofar as it proceeds from his *reason* and *the will* (reason's appetite). Human actions are deliberate actions. Other, nondeliberate (or mindless or accidental) actions are not, properly speaking, human actions but rather "actions of a man" (*ST* I-II, q. 1, a. 1). Examples of such nondeliberate actions would include mindlessly scratching one's beard or twitching one's foot (*ST* I-II, q. 1, a. 1, obj. 3). Because of their rational nature, human persons can move themselves to an end (*ST* I-II, q. 1, a. 2).

Although the end is last in the order of execution (i.e., the goal of an action), the end is first in the order of an agent's intention (*ST* I-II, q. 1, a. 1, ad 1). Intending an end is the reason why a human acts. A human person acts for the sake of a preconceived, desired, and intended end (*ST* I-II, q. 1, a. 3, ad 2). Thus, "the principle of human acts, in so far as they are human, is the end." Additionally, the end is the "terminus" of human action, "for the human act terminates at that which the will intends as the end" (*ST* I-II, q. 1, a. 3). Here, the inescapable importance of the end is readily seen: Without an end, an action would never begin nor would it ever finish. The end is the reason why an action begins. The end is also the concluding term of every action.

Aquinas is most intent to demonstrate that there must be one, single *ultimate* (or last) end of human activity. "Absolutely speaking, it is not possible to proceed indefinitely in the matter of ends, from any point of view" (*ST* I-II, q. 1, a. 4). There must be a single starting point for all of human action. Multiple "last ends" are impossible—one end is always supreme and ultimate (*ST* I-II, q. 1, a. 5).

Consequently, "man must, of necessity, desire all, whatsoever he desires, for the last end" (*ST* I-II, q. 1, a. 6). Aquinas explains that the primacy of the last end is necessary "because whatever man desires, he desires it under the aspect of good. And if he desires it, not as his perfect good, which is the last end, he must, of necessity, desire it as tending to the perfect good"—as ordered to the final end (*ST* I-II, q. 1, a. 6). The human person's ultimate quest for the perfect good is true even when he or she is not presently "thinking of the last end" when they desire or do something (*ST* I-II, q. 6, a. 6, ad 3).

All humans act for the sake of the final end, and all human persons pursue their final end under the same aspect: "all desire the fulfillment of their perfection, and it is precisely this fulfillment in which the last end consists" (*ST* I-II, q. 1, a. 7). It is impossible for human persons to act from any other intention than attainment of the good. Nonetheless, not all humans are in agreement about where the ultimate good resides or how to achieve it: For example, some people "desire riches as their consummate good; some, pleasure; others, something else" (*ST* I-II, q. 1, a. 7).

Thus, the saint and the sinner equally share the orientation to ultimate goodness as their final end. They differ, however, on how the final end of ultimate goodness is to be achieved. "Those who sin turn from that in which their last end really consists: but they do not turn away from the intention of the last end, which intention they mistakenly seek in other things" (*ST* I-II, q. 1, a. 7, ad 1).

Happiness (or Beatitude): Man's Last End in Particular (*ST* I-II, qq. 2–5)

In *ST* I-II, q. 2, Aquinas proceeds to examine whether ultimate happiness (or beatitude) can reside in any created good. And he concludes with absolute certitude that "it is impossible for any created good to constitute man's happiness" (*ST* I-II, q. 2, a. 8). The happiness of beatitude is the "perfect good." And the perfect good, alone, can satisfy the human desire for happiness. Why? "The object of the will"—the will's "objective"—is "the universal good; just as the object of the intellect is the universal true." Thus, the will is not satisfied by any good thing that is not universally good—infinitely good, good in every respect. And this goodness "is to be found, not in any creature, but in God alone; because every creature has goodness by participation" only. God alone is infinitely good. "Therefore God alone constitutes man's happiness" (*ST* I-II, q. 2, a. 8).

All created goods (e.g., wealth, honor, fame, power, health, pleasure, etc.) are limited and derivative goods because of their contingent nature (*ST* I-II, q. 2, aa. 2–8). No created thing is infinite, nor is it ultimate. Each created thing is ordered to something else—the ultimate good.

After Aquinas has proven that all humans act for the sake of an end and that the ultimate end cannot be any created good, he investigates the nature of beatific happiness itself. He explains that "man's last end is the uncreated good, namely God, Who alone by His infinite goodness can perfectly satisfy man's will." Nonetheless, "man's last end is something created" insofar as it exists *in him*. Because the human person is a creature, the human attainment of the uncreated good is creaturely in character. "If, therefore, we consider man's happiness in its cause or object, then it is something uncreated; but if we consider it as to the very essence of happiness, then it is something created" (*ST* I-II, q. 3, a. 1).

Consequently, beatific happiness is an *operation*. Because this happiness is "man's supreme perfection," and "each thing is perfect in so far as it is actual," it follows that this "happiness must consist in man's last [or 'ultimate'] act" (*ST* I-II, q. 3, a. 2). God is beatific happiness *essentially*, "since His very Being is His operation, whereby He enjoys no other than Himself" (*ST* I-II, q. 3, a. 2, ad 4). As creatures, however, the ultimate perfection of the human person is "in respect of an operation whereby man is united to God" (*ST* I-II, q. 3, a. 2, ad 4). In other words, human persons are made happy through *active* union with God (through an operation) while remaining different from God.

Aquinas then investigates which of the powers of the human person is activated, or operative, in beatific union with God, the "Uncreated Good." Because God is not material or particular but is instead spiritual and universal, "the operation whereby man's mind is united to God will not depend on the senses" (*ST* I-II, q. 3, a. 3).

Moreover, "the attainment of the end does not consist in the very act of the will." Why? "The will is directed to the end, both absent, when it desires [the end]; and present, when it is delighted by resting therein" (*ST* I-II, q. 3, a. 3). To desire the end signifies that the end is not present. We do not desire what we fully possess. The will, thus, anticipates the end and rejoices in the end; but the will is not the power of beatific union with the end. Therefore, Aquinas concludes that the "essence of happiness consists in an act of the intellect; but the delight that results from happiness pertains to the will" (*ST* I-II, q. 3, a. 3). Indeed, "the last and perfect happiness, which we await in the life to come, consists entirely in contemplation" (*ST* I-II, q. 3, a. 4). The contemplative act of the intellect possesses the good within the intellect (*ST* I-II, q. 3, a. 4, ad 2).

Hence, "final and perfect happiness can consist in nothing else than the vision of the Divine Essence" (*ST* I-II, q. 3, a. 8). No other object of contemplation—not even the highest sciences, not even the angels—can render the human person finally and perfectly happy (*ST* I-II, q. 3, aa.

6–7). Because the objective of the intellect is "the essence of a thing," the intellect is perfected through knowing what things are. "Consequently, for perfect happiness the intellect needs to reach the very Essence of the First Cause. And thus it will have its perfection through union with God as with that object, in which alone man's happiness consists" (*ST* I-II, q. 3, a. 8).

In sum, perfect happiness—beatitude—is intellectual union with the ultimate good. And this ultimate good is God himself. Contemplating the divine essence alone renders the human person beatifically happy. No other being and no other act can satisfy the deepest longings of the human person.

The Requirements of Happiness (ST *I-II, q. 4)*

Aquinas then turns his attention to what happiness requires. He explains that three things "must concur with Happiness; to wit, vision, which is perfect knowledge of the intelligible end; comprehension, which implies presence of the end; and delight or enjoyment, which implies repose of the lover in the object beloved" (*ST* I-II, q. 4, a. 3).

The intellectual *vision* of the divine essence leads to delightful "repose of the will" (*ST* I-II, q. 4, a. 2). *Comprehension* is necessary for beatitude because such happiness implies "the holding of something already present and possessed: thus one who runs after another is said to comprehend him when he lays hold of him" (*ST* I-II, q. 4, a. 3, ad 1). *Delight* is a requirement for happiness because "it is caused by the appetite being at rest in the good attained. Wherefore, since happiness is nothing else but the attainment of the Sovereign Good, it cannot be without concomitant delight" (*ST* I-II, q. 4, a. 1). It is impossible to see God and not delight in him (*ST* I-II, q. 4, a. 1, ad 2).

Aquinas explains that *rectitude of the will* is also a requirement of beatitude for two reasons. First, "none can obtain Happiness, without rectitude of the will" because "rectitude of the will consists in being duly ordered to the last end" (*ST* I-II, q. 4, a. 4). In the absence of this rectitude, one is not ordered to the ultimate good and thus cannot obtain the ultimate good. Second, when someone enjoys the vision of the divine essence, "the will of him who sees the Essence of God, of necessity, loves, whatever he loves, in subordination to God" (*ST* I-II, q. 4, a. 4). And this correctly ordered love is precisely what rectitude of the will means.

With regard to the body, Aquinas shows that it is not essentially or absolutely required for the happiness of heaven. Because the beatific vision is an intellectual operation, "without the body the soul can be happy" (*ST* I-II, q. 4, a. 5). Nonetheless, the union of the body is required for the "well-being" (or "being well") of the soul's nature. The soul is meant to be united to the body. Thus, "happiness does not consist in bodily good as its object: but bodily good can add a certain charm and perfection to Happiness" insofar as the happiness of the soul will "overflow" to the perfection of the body (*ST* I-II, q. 4, a. 6, ad 1).

The imperfect happiness of this life (i.e., happiness that falls short of the beatific vision) requires *external goods* such as food and possessions, but these goods do not contribute to the essence of happiness. Rather, they serve as "instruments to happiness" (*ST* I-II, q. 4, a. 7). The virtuous, rightly ordered human person requires bodily necessities in order to live. Thus, while material possessions are not essential to perfect happiness, they serve the human pursuit of the supreme good.

Finally, Aquinas asks whether *friends* are required for happiness. "If we speak of the happiness of this life, the happy man needs friends." Why? "For the purpose of good operation," namely, "that he may do good to them, that he may delight in seeing them do good; and again that he may be helped by them in his good work" (*ST* I-II, q. 4, a. 8). Although friends are not essential to the happiness of heaven—"since man has the entire fulness of his perfection in God"—Aquinas concludes that "the fellowship of friends conduces to the well-being of Happiness" (*ST* I-II, q. 4, a. 8).

*The Attainment of Happiness (*ST *I-II, q. 5)*

Given the sublimity of beatific happiness, Aquinas understandably considers what is required for the attainment of the vision of divine essence. He explains, first, that it is truly possible to attain the "Perfect Good." Because the human intellect "can apprehend the universal and perfect good, and because his will can desire it," man is truly capable of arriving at the ultimate end. The fundamental orientation of nature is never in vain. Thus, essential orientation of the rational soul to universal goodness is not in vain.

Although all human persons share the same end—God, the ultimate good—they do not all experience identical levels of the "attainment or enjoyment of that same Good." Thus, in a sense, "one man can be happier than another" in the vision of the divine essence. For those who are "better disposed or ordered to the enjoyment of Him" actually do enjoy God more than those who were less disposed or less well-ordered to the enjoyment of God (*ST* I-II, q. 5, a. 2). Nonetheless, "none of the Blessed lacks any desirable good" absolutely speaking, "since they have the Infinite Good Itself" (*ST* I-II, q. 5, a. 2, ad 3).

With regard to happiness in this life, Aquinas explains that perfect happiness is not possible outside the beatific vision. It is impossible in this life to avoid or exclude every type of evil—and yet evil is inimical to goodness and, consequently, to happiness. "For this present life is subject to many unavoidable evils; to ignorance on the part of the intellect; to inordinate affection on the part of the appetite, and to many penalties on the part of the body" (*ST* I-II, q. 5, a. 3). Additionally, the "specific nature" of beatific happiness is the vision of the divine essence. And the beatific vision is not possible in this life (*ST* I-II, q. 5, a. 3).

Although perfect happiness is not attainable in this life, Aquinas does not believe that it is absolutely miserable. An imperfect happiness is possible and still good—insofar as it is indicative of the virtuous person's order to ultimate happiness. Thus, "some are said to be happy in this life, either on account of the hope of obtaining Happiness in the life to come . . . or on account of a certain participation in Happiness, by reason of a kind of enjoyment of the Sovereign Good" even now, here below (*ST* I-II, q. 5, a. 3).

Although it is absolutely impossible to lose or to forfeit the beatific happiness of the next life, the imperfect happiness of this life is not so secure. Because of complexities of human contingency, the imperfect happiness of this life can be lost. Contemplative happiness can be lost, for example, "when knowledge is lost through sickness" or in the face of "certain occupations, whereby a man is altogether withdrawn from contemplation" (*ST* I-II, q. 5, a. 4). Additionally, the active happiness of this life can also be forfeited if someone succumbs to vice and abandons virtue, "in whose act [active] happiness principally consists" (*ST* I-II, q. 5, a. 4). If one persists in virtue, however, happiness can be hindered or disturbed but never taken completely away.

With regard to the origin of happiness, Aquinas explains that human persons can acquire the imperfect happiness of this life by means of their natural powers (*ST* I-II, q. 5, a. 5). Because of the human person's fundamental orientation to goodness and to perfection, it is possible to acquire virtues naturally. It is absolutely impossible, however, to attain the perfect happiness of heaven by our native and natural capacities alone. "The vision of God's essence surpasses the nature not only of man, but also of every creature" (*ST* I-II, q. 5, a. 5).

Thus, human nature can attain perfect good, "although it needs help from without in order to attain it"—and this help is nothing other than the "Divine assistance" of grace. God alone can help creatures to arrive at him, their supernatural end: "by God alone is man made happy, if we speak of perfect Happiness" (*ST* I-II, q. 5, a. 6). All advancements in our lives toward perfect happiness come from God's initiative. And God's gracious initiative inevitably results in our performance of good works ordered to the vision of the divine essence (*ST* I-II, q. 5, a. 7).

Chapter 8

Actions and Habits

(ST *I-II, qq. 6–89)*

Human action occupies a central place in the *ST* and receives extensive attention throughout its pages. The reason for this centrality is not difficult to recognize. Because "happiness is to be gained by means of certain acts, we must in due sequence consider human acts" (*ST* I-II, q. 6, prol.). Through these words, Aquinas situates the subject of human action in reference to the preceding treatise on man's last end and happiness. And through the subject of happiness, the subject of human action fits into the very opening of the *ST* and the purpose of sacred doctrine (*ST* I, q. 1, a. 7).

Beatific happiness is achieved through human action. Conversely (and tragically), "we are prevented from attaining" this happiness through bad (i.e., disordered) human actions (*ST* I-II, q. 6, prol.). Therefore, human actions stand between the human person and God—as the means through which the person either achieves ultimate union with God or, alternatively, turns away from him.

The study of human action lies at the center of the study of *morals* (*ST* I-II, q. 4, prol.). Harkening back to *ST* I, q. 1, a. 4 ("Whether sacred doctrine is a practical science?"), Aquinas explains that "operations and acts are concerned with things singular, [and] consequently all practical knowledge is incomplete unless it takes account of things" in their singularity and "detail" (*ST* I-II, q. 6, prol.). "The study of morals, therefore, since it treats human acts, should consider first the general principles; and second matters of detail" (*ST* I-II, q. 6, prol.).

Aquinas identifies two general principles of human action: (1) human actions themselves and (2) the principles of human action. Both of these elements are framed in reference to happiness, since it is on account of the incessant quest for happiness that humans act. Consequently, Aquinas is also attuned to what makes human action distinctively human, "since happiness is man's proper good," and "those acts which are proper to man have a closer connection with happiness than have those which are common to man and the other animals" (*ST* I-II, q. 6, prol.).

Aquinas explains that properly human acts are *voluntary* in nature. This means that human acts proceed from the intellect and the will. Not all actions of the human person are voluntary in nature, however. Those acts that are common to humans and nonrational animals are the *passions*. Aquinas devotes attention to both types of action in the *Prima secundae*.

Human Action (*ST* I-II, qq. 6–21)

Aquinas explains that "there must be something voluntary in human acts" (*ST* I-II, q. 6, a. 1). In order to demonstrate the centrality of the voluntary nature of human action, he observes that "the principle of some acts or movements is within the agent," and the principle of other "movements or acts is outside" the agent (*ST* I-II, q. 6, a. 1). To illustrate this distinction, he offers the example of a stone. The movement of a stone *downward* originates from a principle of motion within the stone. It belongs to the nature of a stone to move toward the center of the earth. On the other hand, when a stone moves *upward*, as in the case of being thrown in the air, "the principle of this movement is outside the stone" (*ST* I-II, q. 6, a. 1). Why? Stones do not move themselves upward. Such movement is not natural to them—it does not follow from their nature.

Aquinas then homes in on those types of agents or "actors" that act from an interior principle of motion. He points out that some of these agents "move themselves" and others are not self-moving. All agents, however, act for the sake of an end. As we saw in the previous chapter, there is no such thing as an "end-less being." All things are oriented to an end. Likewise for all actions. "Those are perfectly moved by an intrinsic principle, whose intrinsic principle is one not only of movement but of movement for an end" (*ST* I-II, q. 6, a. 1).

Consequently, self-moving agents that move for the sake of an end from an intrinsic principle of motion have some knowledge of the end for which they move. "Those things which have a knowledge of the end are said to move themselves because there is in them a principle by which they not only act but also act for an end." It is here that the nature of *voluntary* movement or action comes to the fore. Voluntary agents act from an intrinsic principle of action for the sake of an end. Consequently, "since man especially knows the end of his work, and moves himself, in his acts especially is the voluntary to be found" (*ST* I-II, q. 6, a. 1).

Human persons act voluntarily because they can possess *perfect knowledge* of the end. "Perfect knowledge of the end consists in not only apprehending the thing which is the end, but also in knowing it under the aspect of end, and the relationship of the means to that end" (*ST* I-II, q. 6, a. 2). This type of knowledge belongs only to beings of a rational nature. Knowledge is essential to the voluntary: "Voluntariness requires an act of knowledge in the same way as it requires an act of will; namely in order that it be in one's power to consider, to wish and to act" (*ST* I-II, q. 6, a. 3, ad 3).

Nonrational animals also act for the sake of an end but incompletely and thus *imperfectly*. "Imperfect knowledge of the end consists in mere apprehension of the end, without knowing it under the aspect of end, or the relationship of an act to the end. Such knowledge of the end is exercised by irrational animals, through their senses and their estimative power" (*ST* I-II, q. 6, a. 2). The perfectly voluntary arises from the fact that a man not only apprehends an end but also deliberates "about the end and the means thereto," and "can be moved, or not, to gain the end." For the imperfectly voluntary, "the agent apprehends the end, but does not deliberate, and is moved to the end at once" (*ST* I-II, q. 6, a. 2). This explains why man is considered the "master of his actions" (*ST* I-II, q. 6, a. 2, ad 2) and why "praise and blame are the result of the voluntary act . . . such as is not to be found in irrational animals" (*ST* I-II, q. 6, a. 2, ad 3).

Aquinas explains that God can move the human person to act "by moving the will itself" (*ST* I-II, q. 6, a. 1, ad 3). Created causes, however, affect the will in a less intimate way—externally, as it were. There are two kinds of acts of the will. The first is called an *elicited act* of the will. This is the act of the will itself and can be described as "to wish." The second type of act of the will is a *commanded act*. Commanded acts are those that are "put into execution by means of some other power, such as *to walk* and *to speak*" (*ST* I-II, q. 6, a. 4; italics in the original). The commanded acts are voluntary insofar as they truly follow from an act of the will. But these commanded acts of walking and speaking are not *exclusively* voluntary in the sense that an act of the will is insufficient to accomplish the acts of walking and speaking—there must be physical movement involved as well: These acts are "commanded by the will," but they are "executed by means of the motive power" (*ST* I-II, q. 6, a. 4).

In sum, Aquinas's presentation of human action recognizes the centrality of the intellect and the will. Human action is voluntary action. It arises from the rational nature of the human person—the capacity to understand an end and to act for that end.

End and Means

The will is moved both to the end and to the means ordered to the end (*ST* I-II, q. 8, prol.). Both movements fall under the fundamental orientation of the will to the good. All appetites are inclined to the good (*ST* I-II, q. 8, a. 1). As the rational appetite, the will is inclined to the rationally apprehended good. The good of the end enjoys primacy in the acts of the will. Indeed, "volition is of the end only" (*ST* I-II, q. 8, a. 2).

Means without an end are unintelligible. Means—as such—are only means ordered to some end. Of course, as a power, the will "extends both to the end and the means" (*ST* I-II, q. 8, a. 3). But "the means are good and willed, not in themselves, but as referred to the end. Wherefore the will is directed to them, only insofar as [the will] is directed to the end: so that what it wills in them, is the end" (*ST* I-II, q. 8, a. 2). Consequently, it is possible for the will to be "moved to the end, without being moved to the means." The inverse, however, is not possible. The will "cannot be moved to the means, as such, unless it is moved to the end" (*ST* I-II, q. 8, a. 3).

In sum, the end—and the will's intended order to the end—is the foundation of all human action. Aquinas is very clear: The will *intends* the end and *chooses* the means in reference to the intended end (*ST* I-II, q. 12, and *ST* I-II, q. 13). This precise order between ends and means is absolutely essential for an intelligible and consistent account of human action. All human actions arise from the intention of an end—even those human actions that are intermediate actions (i.e., means) ordered to an end. Human action only exists in reference to an end, and it is only intelligible in reference to that end.

Good and Evil Actions

Although all humans act for the sake of some good, not all human actions are morally good. There is such a thing as evil action (*ST* I-II,

q. 18, a. 1). The distinction between good and evil actions is grounded in the fact that evil human actions fundamentally lack a requisite good element. "We must therefore say that every action has goodness, insofar as it has being; whereas it is lacking in goodness, insofar as it is lacking in something that is due to its fullness of being; and thus it is said to be evil" (*ST* I-II, q. 18, a. 1).

Because "the good or evil of an action . . . depends on the fulness of being or its lack of fulness," the *being* of an action determines whether an action is good or evil. An action's being arises from three constitutive elements: the *object*, *circumstances*, and *end*. In order for an act to be morally good, all three of these must be good. An act is morally evil, however, if it lacks even one of these three elements.

Aquinas explains, "A fourfold goodness may be considered in a human action. First, that which, as an action, it derives from its genus; because as much as it has of action and being so much has it of goodness." Because it is better to be than not to be, an action is good insofar as it exists. Nonetheless, a human action secondly "has goodness according to its species; which is derived from its suitable object. Third, it has goodness from its circumstances, in respect, as it were, of its accidents. Fourth, it has goodness from its end, to which it is compared as to the cause of its goodness" (*ST* I-II, q. 18, a. 4).

The *object* of an action refers to the generic kind of action that it is. The object gives an action its *species*. "Just as the primary goodness of a natural thing is derived from its form, which gives it its species, so the primary goodness of a moral action is derived from its suitable object" (*ST* I-II, q. 18, a. 2). *Right reason* is the standard by which the moral quality of the object is determined (*ST* I-II, q. 18, a. 5). A human action is morally good "inasmuch as it is in accord with reason, and evil, inasmuch as it is against reason" (*ST* I-II, q. 18, a. 5, ad 1). Aquinas offers as an example of a moral object *taking what belongs to another*. Reason can recognize that this action is not perfective of the human person and of human society. Theft is harmful. It is objectively disordered.

The *circumstance* of a human act "is described as something outside the substance of the act, and yet in a way touching it" (*ST* I-II, q. 7, a. 3). Circumstances are "the particular conditions" of an act (*ST* I-II, q. 7, a. 1, s.c.). They are contextual qualities that particularize an action. Quoting Aristotle, Aquinas explains that "a virtuous man acts as he should, and when he should, and so on in respect of the other circumstances."

Conversely, "the vicious man, in the matter of each vice, acts when he should not, or where he should not, and so on with the other circumstances" (*ST* I-II, q. 18, a. 3, s.c.). Although circumstances are "outside an action, inasmuch as they are not part of its essence," they are nevertheless "in an action as accidents therefore" (*ST* I-II, q. 18, a. 3). Circumstances can compromise the goodness of a human action even if the object of the action is good. (For example, telling wholesome and amusing jokes is objectively good, but telling such jokes in the middle of a funeral liturgy would be disordered and bad.)

Finally, the *end* is also significant in the moral quality of a given human action. The end—the object of the interior act of the will—accounts for the very existence of the action (*ST* I-II, q. 18, a. 7). The end explains why an action is performed, why it exists. Therefore, a morally disordered motivation—giving rise to the action itself—can compromise an objectively good action, even one performed in suitable circumstances.

The Passions (*ST* I-II, qq. 22–48)

Not all actions of the human person are voluntary in nature. In other words, not all actions follow from the deliberation of reason. Some actions are *passions*. These types of actions are common to both rational animals (i.e., the human person) and nonrational animals (e.g., the cat, the dog).

The word "passion" indicates a kind of change that takes place in the *sensitive powers* (*ST* I-II, q. 22, a. 3). Today, we would call the passions *emotions*. There are two sensitive (or "sense") power appetites: the concupiscible and the irascible (*ST* I, q. 81, a. 2; *ST* I-II, q. 23, a. 1).

The object of the concupiscible appetite is "sensible good or evil, simply apprehended as such, which causes pleasure or pain" (*ST* I-II, q. 23, a. 1). The object of the irascible appetite is "an arduous or difficult" good or evil. Aquinas continues, "Therefore whatever passions regard good or evil absolutely, belong to the concupiscible power . . . whereas those passions which regard good or bad as arduous, through being difficult to obtain or avoid, belong to the irascible" power (*ST* I-II, q. 23, a. 1).

The whole of human activity arises from the nature of the good. Thus, Aquinas distinguishes the passions in reference to the sensible goods that move the human person in different ways. "Good has, as it were, a force of attraction, while evil has a force of repulsion." From this universal observation, Aquinas proceeds to parse the different passions of the concupiscible appetite. "In the first place, therefore, good causes, in the appetitive power, a certain inclination, aptitude or connaturalness [a kind of 'second-naturedness'] in respect of good: and this belongs to the passion of *love*: the corresponding contrary of which is *hatred* in respect of evil" (*ST* I-II, q. 23, a. 4). These are the fundamental passions. They regard the good (and its privation, evil), absolutely speaking.

With regard to a "good not yet possessed," there is a movement in the sense appetites *toward* the good—so as to possess it. The movement toward the sensible good not yet possessed is called *desire* or *concupiscence*. The movement away from an evil coming but not yet present is called *aversion* or *dislike*.

Finally, with regard to a good possessed, there is the passion of *delight* or *joy*; and with regard to a present evil, the passion of *sorrow* or *sadness*.

The irascible passions follow upon and presuppose the concupiscible power, which "regards good or evil absolutely" (*ST* I-II, q. 23, a. 4). In the case of "a good not yet obtained," there are the passions of *hope* and *despair*. The object of hope is a future good that is difficult but possible to obtain (*ST* I-II, q. 40, a. 1). Despair is a movement of withdrawal from an unobtainable good (*ST* I-II, q. 40, a. 4). In the case of an "evil not yet present," there are the passions of *fear* and *daring*. The object of fear is a future evil that is "difficult and irresistible" (*ST* I-II, q. 41, a. 2). Although fear turns away from a future evil, daring turns toward the future evil "because of its own victory over that same danger" (*ST* I-II, q. 45, a. 1).

Finally, in the case of an evil already present, there is the passion of *anger*. There is no irascible passion for a good obtained, because a good obtained is "no longer considered in the light of something arduous"—and arduousness is the aspect that unifies the passions of the irascible faculty (*ST* I-II, q. 23, a. 4).

In sum, "there are altogether eleven passions differing specifically; six in the concupiscible faculty, and five in the irascible; and under these all the passions of the soul are contained" (*ST* I-II, q. 23, a. 4).

The Morality of the Passions

Unlike human (i.e., voluntary) actions, "there is no moral good or evil" in the passions "considered in themselves" (*ST* I-II, q. 24, a. 1). Aquinas emphasizes the fact that the rational appetite, or the will, and the sensitive appetite are really distinct appetites (*ST* I-II, q. 24, a. 2). Moral goodness and moral evil are voluntary in nature. Consequently, the passions are morally good or evil insofar as they are voluntary. "And they are said to be voluntary either from being commanded by the will or from not being checked by the will" (*ST* I-II, q. 24, a. 1). And because the will is reason's appetite, "the passions of the soul, insofar as they are contrary to the order of reason, incline us to sin: but insofar as they are controlled by reason, they pertain to virtue" (*ST* I-II, q. 24, a. 2, ad 3).

Aquinas is emphatic that the passions are not intrinsically evil. Moreover, he rejects all philosophies that characterize bodily pleasure as bad. "None can live without some sensible and bodily pleasure" (*ST* I-II, q. 34, a. 1). Feelings alone do not specify moral behavior. Indeed, feelings are good. The real issue is what we do with our feelings—how we order our feelings under the influence of right reason. The virtuous person directs their entire being—thoughts, decisions, and feelings—according to the order of right reason. Indeed, the passions are subject to the direction of the intellect and the will. The human person is essentially united. Therefore, it is possible for the human person to operate in an integrated way. The sense appetites, themselves, can be virtuously ordered—according to right reason.

Habits (*ST* I-II, qq. 49–89)

After Aquinas provides an overview of human action and the passions, he "pass[es] on to the consideration of the principles of human acts" (*ST* I-II, q. 49, prol.). There are two groupings of the principles of human action: *intrinsic* and *extrinsic*.

The intrinsic principles of human action are the *powers* of the human person—for example, the intellectual and the appetitive—and the *habits* (*habitus*, in Latin) that shape these human powers. The powers themselves received Aquinas's attention in the *Prima pars* (*ST* I, qq. 77–83). The *Prima secundae*, therefore, turns its attention to habits (*ST* I-II, qq. 49–89).

A habit is a kind of quality (*ST* I-II, q. 49, a. 1). Specifically, it is a stable disposition that shapes a power. Habits are not easily lost (*ST* I-II, q. 49, a. 2). The stability of habits is essential to their definition, which is why habits are principles of action. Powers act. A habit within a power is a stable disposition that orders that power toward a specific kind of action. Consequently, Aquinas explains that habit "implies a disposition in relation to a thing's nature, and to its operation or end, by reason of which disposition a thing is well or ill disposed thereto" (*ST* I-II, q. 49, a. 4).

Virtue, Vice, and the Gifts of the Holy Spirit

Habits can shape different kinds of powers of the human person. The sensitive powers, the intellect, and the will can all receive habitual shaping (*ST* I-II, q. 50, aa. 3–5). "Every power which may be variously directed to act, needs a habit whereby it is well disposed to its act" (*ST* I-II, q. 50, a. 5). And because the sensitive powers, the intellect, and the will can all be activated for diverse objects (some perfective, others defective), they are subject to habitual shaping. Habits that perfectively shape a power are called *virtues*—these are "good" habits. Those habits that defectively shape a power are called *vices*—"bad" habits. They harm the power and, consequently, the human person whose nature possesses that power.

The distinction between the goodness and badness of different habits arises from their respective "suitableness or unsuitableness to nature. In this way a good habit is specifically distinct from a bad habit: since a good habit is one which disposes to an act suitable to the agent's nature, while an evil habit is one which disposes to an act unsuitable to nature." Hence, "acts of virtue are suitable to human nature," and "acts of vice are discordant from human nature" (*ST* I-II, q. 54, a. 3). This is why the habit of "virtue denotes a certain perfection of a power," and a vicious habit denotes a certain defection of a power (*ST* I-II, q. 55, a. 1). Because a habit gives "actional shape" to a power, we can say that a habit stands as a midway point between the state of potentiality and the state of actuality. A habit imprints within a power the shape of an act (i.e., perfective and virtuous, or defective and vicious) even when the power is not presently acting.

On a natural level, there is such a thing as *acquired habits*. These habits shape the powers of the human person through repeated activity (*ST* I-II, q. 63, a. 2). We can naturally act in a way that perfects the powers of our nature, or we can act in a way that harms the powers of our nature. Therefore, our deliberate and repeated actions can shape our powers of action. Examples of acquired virtue include the *intellectual virtues* (*ST* I-II, q. 57) and the *moral virtues* (*ST* I-II, q. 58). The intellectual virtues perfect the intellect in the different ways of knowing the truth because truth is the good of the intellect (*ST* I-II, q. 57, a. 1). The moral virtues perfect the appetitive powers of the human person. "For a man to do a good deed, it is requisite not only that his reason be well disposed by means of a habit of intellectual virtue; but also that his appetite be well disposed by means of a habit of moral virtue" (*ST* I-II, q. 58, a. 2). Possessing *rational* and *sensitive* appetites, the human person can shape both (*ST* I-II, q. 59). The will and the passions can therefore receive the perfective ordering of virtuous habits.

In order to flourish holistically, the human person requires intellectual as well as moral virtues. "Human virtue is a habit perfecting man in view of his doing good deeds." Thus, because "in man there are but two principles of human actions, viz., the intellect or reason and the appetite," the human person requires the habitual perfection of each of these principles, or powers, in order to achieve goodness. And because the human person is essentially one, the human person requires the perfection of both intellectual and moral virtue (*ST* I-II, q. 58, aa. 4–5).

Beyond the acquired virtues, there are also *infused habits* (*ST* I-II, q. 63, a. 3). These virtues arise from the shaping influence of grace. The infused habits are virtues ordered to God as to our "supernatural end" (*ST* I-II, q. 63, a. 3). Rather than being acquired through repeated action, infused habits are given by God to the human person through grace. The theological virtues (*ST* I-II, q. 62) and the infused moral virtues (*ST* I-II, q. 63, a. 3, ad 2) are preeminent examples of such habits. (Aquinas considers these habits at length in the *Secunda secundae*.)

In addition to the infused virtues—the theological virtues and the infused moral virtues—there are also the infused habits of the *gifts of the Holy Spirit*. The gifts of the Holy Spirit are infused habits that render the human person subject to the direct "inspiration" of God (*ST* I-II, q. 68, a. 1). "The gifts are perfections of man, whereby he is disposed so as to be amenable to the promptings of God. Wherefore in those matters where the prompting of [human] reason is not sufficient, and there is need for the prompting of the Holy Spirit, there is, in consequence, need for a gift" (*ST* I-II, q. 68, a. 2).

The integration of the acquired virtues and the infused virtues—both moral and theological—as well as the gifts of the Holy Spirit and the Beatitudes, is the focus of the following section of the *ST*, the *Secunda secundae*.

Chapter 9

Law and Grace

(ST I-II, qq. 90–114)

In the prologue to *ST* I-II, q. 90, Aquinas explains that the *ST* will now consider the extrinsic principles of human action. These principles are called extrinsic (or "external") not because they have no influence within the soul but because they originate from a source outside of the human person.

Interestingly, the extrinsic principles of human action are *personal principles*: namely, *God* and the *devil*. Because a *principle* is that from which something proceeds in any way, Aquinas considers what proceeds from the devil and from God. The devil, he says, *inclines* us to evil. God, however, *moves* us to the good.

Unsurprisingly, God's influence on human action is deeper—more intimate—than that of the devil. The reason for the profundity of God's influence on human action is the intimacy of *divine providence*. As we saw in chapter 6, the God who creates also orders what he creates. And he orders his creation even in the very depths of his created being.

God moves his creatures to the perfective good in two ways: through *law* and *grace*. Through law, God *instructs* us in what is good. Through grace, he *helps* us to achieve the good. Thus, law has a pedagogical nature, leading its recipients to their proper virtue (*ST* I-II, q. 92, a. 1). And grace has an auxiliary nature, enabling its recipients to exist and to act in a supernatural way. Therefore, these sections of the *ST* address the following topics:

- Section 1: *ST* I-II, qq. 90–108: God *instructing* through *law*
- Section 2: *ST* I-II, qq. 109–114: God *helping* through *grace*

God Instructing Through Law (*ST* I-II, qq. 90–108)

Aquinas's theological examination of the law is divided into two parts: *general* and *specific*. The general and universal nature of law receives consideration in *ST* I-II, qq. 90–92, and the particular types of law are delineated in *ST* I-II, qq. 93–108.

*Law in General (*ST *I-II, qq. 90–92)*

Aquinas explains that "three points offer themselves for our consideration [of the nature of law]: (1) Its essence; (2) The different kinds of law; (3) The effects of law" (*ST* I-II, q. 90, prol.).

Aquinas offers a concise definition of law in the first question of this treatise: "[Law] is nothing else than an ordinance of reason for the common good, made by him who has care of the community, and promulgated" (*ST* I-II, q. 90, a. 4). Law bespeaks order, and order formally belongs to the intellect—the power that recognizes and formulates order. The inherent rationality of law resides in the function that reason plays in human action. "It belongs to law to command and to forbid." The act of commanding, however, is a rational act—"it belongs to reason to command." "Therefore," Aquinas concludes, "law is something pertaining to reason" (*ST* I-II, q. 90, a. 1, s.c.).

Aquinas reminds his readers that the first principle of human action is reason. As we saw in the previous chapter, authentically human action is rational in nature. Rational intention and deliberation inform human action. Consequently, reason rules and measures human action because reason is the power that recognizes and instills order. Reason "directs to the end" (*ST* I-II, q. 90, a. 1, ad 1). All order is reasonable. All disorder is contrary to right reason. Therefore, law is rational in nature.

The *ST* explains that law resides in something in two ways: actively and passively. *Actively*, it exists in reason as that which imparts ruling and measuring order, and *passively*, in that which is ruled or measured by reason. Anytime there is reason, there is also order. And anytime there is order, there is also law.

In *ST* I-II, q. 90, a. 2, Aquinas links reason and human action to the ultimate importance of the last end. We recall from chapter 7 that the final end serves as the first principle of human action. Law, as a rule of human action, is ordered to virtue and to the final end. Consequently, happiness is not something exclusively individualistic in nature. Rather, Aquinas says that "the law must needs regard properly the relationship to common happiness." This shared order to common happiness lies at the heart of the common good's importance. Indeed, "every law is ordained to the common good."

Because the law regards "first and foremost the order to the common good," it is not surprising that only "public personages"—those who have "care of the whole people"—can make a law. No one can act in public beyond their proper role and place in the public. Finally, promulgation is essential to authentic law because law rules or measures. And no one can act in accord with legal rule or measure if they lack knowledge of this rule or measure. Consequently, there is no such thing as a completely private or "secret" law. Such secrecy would contradict the inherent rationality of law.

*Particular Kinds of Law (*ST *I-II, qq. 93–108)*

The Eternal Law (*ST* I-II, q. 93)

The first—and foundational—law that Aquinas considers is the *eternal law*. Simply defined, the eternal law is *how God knows the world to be*. Thus, the eternal law exists in the divine intellect. It also exists in creatures, as they are created according to the knowledge of the divine intellect. Indeed, the eternal law is impressed upon the very being, nature, and inclinations of all creatures—animate and inanimate, rational and nonrational.

Consequently, the eternal law can be said to exist both in God and in the creature. It exists in God insofar as it is the divine ideas (or "types") of the things he has created and ordered, and it exists in creatures insofar as they exist in conformity to the ideas God has in his mind about them.

From the universality of the eternal law, Aquinas then shows that every law is, necessarily, derived from the eternal law (*ST* I-II, q. 93, a. 3). All law is ordered to the good, to order, to perfective fulfillment; in other words, to the end. And divine reason establishes order, inclination, and perfective fulfillment in all of reality.

The Natural Law (*ST* I-II, q. 94)

All beings participate passively in the eternal law, while rational creatures—human persons and the angels—participate in it both passively and actively. Therefore, the tree, the bird, the human being, and the angel all passively participate in the eternal law. However, it is only the rational creature—the angels and the human person—that understand their passive participation in the eternal law. Rational creatures can understand order *as order*. Therefore, they can recognize that they exist according to an order—one derived from the divine intellect. In other words, rational creatures can think God's thoughts after him.

The rational creature's participation in the eternal law is called the *natural law*. Indeed, the natural law is identical with the eternal law in the order of *being*. The natural law differs from the eternal law insofar as the natural law is a specifically rational and active participation in the eternal law. Therefore, the distinction between the eternal law and the natural law is not one of substance but rather one of cognition.

All natural law precepts follow upon the first principle of practical (i.e., "action-al") reason: "good is to be done and pursued, and evil is to be avoided" (*ST* I-II, q. 94, a. 2). The desirability of goodness is self-evident. Everyone, ultimately, seeks goodness. All things are *inclined* to the good. Thus, "all other precepts of the natural law are based upon this: so that whatever the practical reason naturally apprehends as man's good (or evil) belongs to the precepts of the natural law as something to be done or avoided" (*ST* I-II, q. 94, a. 2).

When goodness and its order are understood, reason simultaneously recognizes the fundamental inclinations of human nature. The first natural law inclination is ordered to the goodness of being: "every substance seeks the preservation of its own being, according to its nature: and by reason of this inclination, whatever is a means of preserving human life and of warding off its obstacles, belongs to the natural law" (*ST* I-II, q. 94, a. 2). The natural law inclination to preserve one's being and existence is shared with all things.

Reason can also recognize that "there is in man an inclination to things that pertain to him more specially, according to that nature which he has in common with other animals." This natural law inclination is ordered to the preservation of the *species*. Concretely, this inclination is expressed in "sexual intercourse, [and in the] education of offspring and so forth" (*ST* I-II, q. 94, a. 2).

Finally, reason can recognize in the human person "an inclination to good, according to the nature of his reason. Unlike existence (shared with all things) and reproduction (shared with all animals), this inclination "is proper to him: thus man has a natural inclination to know the truth about God, and to live in society" (*ST* I-II, q. 94, a. 2). To know the truth about God and to live in society depend upon rationality. Therefore, these inclinations are proper to rational creatures.

Again, these three natural law inclinations and precepts all follow upon the first precept of the natural law. "All these precepts of the law of nature have the character of one natural law inasmuch as they flow from the one first precept, namely, do good and avoid evil" (*ST* I-II, q. 94, a. 2, ad 1). Thus, in the first precept of practical reason, the natural law has a certain unity.

Human Law (*ST* I-II, qq. 95–97)

Human law (or "positive law") is derived from the natural law: "Every human law has just as much of the nature of law, as it is derived from the law of nature. But if in any point it deflects from the law of nature, it is no longer a law but a perversion of law" (*ST* I-II, q. 95, a. 2).

Human law is a work of reason that extends the general precepts of the natural law to particular matters and circumstances. It is ordered to just and harmonious relations between human persons. "In human affairs a thing is said to be just, from being right, according to the rule of reason" (*ST* I-II, q. 95, a. 2). Human law necessarily follows upon the natural law because "the general principles of the natural law cannot be applied to all men in the same way on account of the great variety of human affairs." Human reason recognizes this great variety and recognizes the need for a "diversity of positive laws among various people" (*ST* I-II, q. 95, a. 2, ad 3).

In sum, the need for positive, human law arises from the fact that no human person is absolutely self-sufficient. "Man has a natural aptitude for virtue; but the perfection of virtue must be acquired by man by means of some kind of training," discipline, or instruction (*ST* I-II, q. 95, a. 1). And "this kind of training, which compels through fear of punishment, is the discipline of laws" (*ST* I-II, q. 95, a. 1). Aquinas cites Isidore's explanation about the necessity of human law: "Laws are made that in fear thereof human audacity may be held in check, that innocence may be safeguarded in the midst of wickedness, and that the dread of punishment might prevent the wicked from doing harm" (*ST* I-II, q. 95, a. 1, s.c.). Thus, human laws forbid "the more grievous vices, from which it is possible for the majority to abstain; and chiefly those that are to the hurt of others, without the prohibition of which human society could not be maintained." The most evident examples of such include "murder, theft and such like" (*ST* I-II, q. 96, a. 2).

Although some things can never be permitted (e.g., murder and theft), the human law can undergo changes in order to facilitate the flourishing of the common good (e.g., traffic laws and taxation). Over time, legal reasoning can recognize that there are better, more efficient ways to order a society (*ST* I-II, q. 97, a. 1). Because the dynamics of civil society can change, human law can change (*ST* I-II, q. 97, a. 1, ad 2).

The Divine Law (*ST* I-II, qq. 98–108)

In addition to the natural law and human law, there is also the divine law. Like both the natural law and human law, moreover, the divine law reflects the order of the eternal law. As we have seen, the natural law and human law are both participations in the eternal law through human reason. Human reason's reflection upon the reality that God has established gives rise to these two kinds of laws. Thus, we can say that natural law and human law are *indirect* participations in the eternal law. Namely, human reason indirectly conforms to the eternal law *through* created things.

In contrast, the divine law is God's *direct* revelation of the eternal law. This is why it is called "divine." Human persons receive the divine law directly from God himself.

Aquinas identifies four reasons why human persons required the divine law in addition to the natural law and to human law:

(1) Because the human person is directed to God as to a supernatural end, "it was necessary that, besides the natural and the human law, man should be directed to his end by a law given by God"—directly (*ST* I-II, q. 91, a. 4).

(2) There are many complexities conjoined to human activity and behavior. Subsequently, it is not easy for human reason to navigate with probity and certainty through all of the complexities of human life. "In order, therefore, that man may know without any doubt what he ought to do and what he ought to avoid, it was necessary for man to be directed in his proper acts by a law given by God, for it is certain that such a law cannot err" (*ST* I-II, q. 91, a. 4).

(3) Human laws can only regulate external human behavior. "Man is not competent to judge of interior movements, that are hidden."

Nonetheless, the interior life is also very important for human flourishing. Therefore, "it was necessary for this purpose that a Divine law should supervene" (*ST* I-II, q. 91, a. 4).

(4) Finally, the range of human law is restricted such that it "cannot punish or forbid all evil deeds." God, however, suffers no such limitations. "In order, therefore, that no evil might remain unforbidden and unpunished, it was necessary for the Divine law to supervene, whereby all sins are forbidden" (*ST* I-II, q. 91, a. 4).

The divine law is divided into the *Old Law* and the *New Law*. The distinction between these two kinds of divine law is that of *imperfection* and *perfection*. As an adult is more "perfect" than a child—insofar as the child is ordered to the perfection of adulthood—the Old Law is imperfect in comparison with the New Law. The New Law is the perfection and the culmination of the Old Law. Thus, the Old Law is ordered to "sensible and earthly good." In contrast, the New Law is ordained to "an intelligible and heavenly good" (*ST* I-II, q. 91, a. 5).

Additionally, "the New Law surpasses the Old Law, since it directs our internal acts," our souls, whereas the Old Law only "restrains the hand" externally (*ST* I-II, q. 91, a. 5). Thus, the New Law can touch on the heart of the human person in a way that the Old Law never could.

Finally, all laws "induce men to observe its commandments." The Old Law accomplished this task "by the fear of punishment." The New Law, however, induces us to observe its commandments through love, "which is poured into our hearts by the grace of Christ" (*ST* I-II, q. 91, a. 5).

The Old Law (*ST* I-II, qq. 98–105)

Although the Old Law was imperfect, it was nonetheless truly good (*ST* I-II, q. 98, a. 1). It was good insofar as it reflected right reason and directed the human person to God—the end of the human person. It was imperfect insofar as it provided "some assistance in attaining the end, but [was] not sufficient for the realization thereof" (*ST* I-II, q. 98, a. 1).

The Old Law is unified insofar as it directed the human person to a single end. There are many Old Law precepts, however, "in respect of the diversity of those things that are ordained to that end" (*ST* I-II, q. 99, a. 2). Thus, Aquinas identifies within the Old Law three groupings of precepts: moral, judicial, and ceremonial.

The *moral precepts* of the Old Law direct human behavior according to right reason. In this respect, the moral precepts of the Old Law are deeply consonant with the natural law. "All the moral precepts of the [Old] Law belong to the law of nature" (*ST* I-II, q. 100, a. 1). Nonetheless, not all of these moral precepts belong to the law of nature in the same way. First, "there are certain things which the natural reason of every man, of its own accord and at once, judges to be done and not to be done," for example, act justly and do not steal. There are other things, however, that require "more careful consideration" and are only recognized by wise persons, such as showing deference to those of advanced age and experience. Finally, "there are some things, to judge of which, human reason needs Divine instruction, whereby we are taught about the things of God," for instance, not taking God's name in vain (*ST* I-II, q. 100, a. 1). The Ten Commandments—the "Decalogue"—are the divine summary of the natural law (*ST* I-II, q. 100, a. 3).

The *ceremonial precepts* of the Old Law "are determinations of the moral precepts whereby man is directed to God." Specifically, these precepts "pertain to the Divine worship" (*ST* I-II, q. 101, a. 1). The ceremonial precepts are primarily about *sacrifices* offered to God in worship and secondarily about everything related to—or done in preparation for—the divine worship (see *ST* I-II, q. 101, a. 4). These Old Law precepts "are ordained to the Divine worship, for that particular time, and to the foreshadowing of time" (*ST* I-II, q. 102, a. 2).

The Old Law's *judicial precepts* concern "man's relations to other men" (*ST* I-II, q. 104, a. 1). There are different types of relation among people. Accordingly, Aquinas identifies a "fourfold order" in the judicial precepts. This comprises the order between (1) a sovereign leader and his subjects, (2) the subjects themselves, (3) a citizen of a state and a foreigner, and (4) the members of a household.

The New Law (*ST* I-II, qq. 106–108)

The New Law is also known as "the Law of the Gospel." It is a law that came with Jesus Christ and retired the structures of the Old Law. The New Law is the fulfillment of the Old. Consequently, the Old Law no longer has salvific currency. Indeed, Aquinas explains that the ceremonial precepts are presently "both dead and deadly"—they are not only ineffectual but also harmful (*ST* I-II, q. 103, a. 4, ad 1). "Now that which is preponderant in the law of the New Testament, and whereon all its efficacy is based, is the grace of the Holy Spirit, which is given through faith in Christ. Consequently, the New Law is chiefly the grace itself of the Holy Spirit, which is given to those who believe in Christ" (*ST* I-II, q. 106, a. 1).

The New Law is "in the first place a law that is inscribed on our hearts," and only secondarily is it a written law (*ST* I-II, q. 106, a. 1). Thus, the New Law not only teaches us what we should do, it also helps us to accomplish it (*ST* I-II, q. 106, a. 1, ad 2). The New Law is a law of complete transformation. It causes the interior change within us that the Old Law never could. The New Law is "the grace of the Holy Spirit bestowed inwardly. And as to this, the New Law justifies" (*ST* I-II, q. 106, a. 2).

While "the Old Law is like a pedagogue of children, as the Apostle says (Gal 3:24)," the New Law is "the law of perfection, since it is the law of charity, of which the Apostle says (Col 3:14) that it is *the bond of perfection*" (*ST* I-II, q. 107, a. 1; italics in the original). The Old Law is the "law of shadow or of figure." The New Law is called the "law of reality"—the law of saving truth (*ST* I-II, q. 107, a. 2).

God Helping Through Grace (*ST* I-II, qq. 109–114)

The transition from the topic of the New Law to the topic of grace is seamless. The New Law is an interior law—a law of freedom. It transforms us inwardly, and "through grace, we are helped by Him to do right" (*ST* I-II, q. 109, prol.). Aquinas divides the five remaining questions of the *Prima secundae* into three parts: (1) the essence of grace, (2) the cause of grace, and (3) the effects of grace.

*The Necessity, Essence, and Division of Grace (*ST *I-II, qq. 109–111)*

Aquinas explains that the human person is naturally ordered to God. Indeed, "to love God above all things is natural to man and to every nature, not only rational but irrational, and even to inanimate nature according to the manner of love which can belong to each creature" (*ST* I-II, q. 109, a. 3). Because God created all things, God is the natural end of all things. Everything is thus inclined to God in a way proportioned to (in a way that "fits") their creaturely natures.

Additionally, while the human person can perform some naturally good works without grace, such as "to build dwellings, plant vineyards, and the like" (*ST* I-II, q. 109, a. 2), no one can "by his natural endowments . . . produce meritorious works proportionate to everlasting life" (*ST* I-II, q. 109, a. 5). Why? God is not only the natural end of the human person—God is also the *supernatural end* of the human person. Everlasting life is beyond the natural reach of human persons and therefore requires God's intervention to achieve.

Aquinas makes a significant distinction between the types of help that God provides. The first type of help is God's *moving assistance*. All creatures require this type of assistance. No creature can absolutely self-actualize. No creature "can proceed to its act unless it be moved by God." Indeed, "every motion is from God as from the First Mover" (*ST* I-II, q. 109, a. 1). And this kind of divine assistance does not imply any inherent supernatural quality in the soul.

With regard to human freedom, Aquinas explains that God even moves the free will: "Man's turning to God is by free-will; and thus man is bidden to turn himself to God. But free-will can only be turned to God, when God turns it" (*ST* I-II, q. 109, a. 6, ad 1).

The second type of divine help is "a habitual gift whereby corrupted human nature is healed, and after being healed is lifted up so as to work deeds meritoriously of everlasting life, which exceeds the capability of nature" (*ST* I-II, q. 109, a. 9). This second type of divine help is *grace* in the common usage of the term. In this sense, grace is a quality inherent in the soul (*ST* I-II, q. 110, a. 2). This "grace, as a quality, is said to act upon the soul, not after the manner of an efficient cause [that moves], but after the manner of a formal cause, as whiteness makes a thing white, and justice, just" (*ST* I-II, q. 110, a. 2, ad 1). Habitual grace resides within the "essence of the soul" (*ST* I-II, q. 110, a. 4).

With regard to the different kinds of grace, Aquinas makes several distinctions. The first distinction is between *sanctifying grace* and *gratuitous grace*. Sanctifying grace is habitual grace. It is the grace "whereby man himself is united to God." Gratuitous grace is "that whereby one man cooperates with another in leading him [the other] to God" (*ST* I-II, q. 111, a. 1). Examples of gratuitous graces include the performance of miracles and the human manifestation of knowledge that "God alone can know" (*ST* I-II, q. 111, a. 4). Aquinas is emphatic, however, that sanctifying grace is higher and "more noble" than gratuitous grace. The reason: The end is always more excellent than the means. "Sanctifying grace ordains a man immediately to a union with his last end, whereas gratuitous grace ordains a man to what is preparatory to the end" (*ST* I-II, q. 111, a. 5).

The second distinction is between *operating grace* and *cooperating grace*. Through operative grace, God unilaterally moves the human person in a supernatural manner. "Hence in that effect in which our mind is moved and does not move, but in which God is the sole mover, the operation is attributed to God" (*ST* I-II, q. 111, a. 2). Cooperative grace refers to cases in which "our mind both moves and is moved, the operation is not only attributed to God, but also to the soul" (*ST* I-II, q. 111, a. 2). Aquinas clarifies that "operating and cooperating are the same grace" (*ST* I-II, q. 111, a. 2, ad 4). Hence, "man is helped by God to will the good, through the means of operating grace." But when the good is "already intended, grace cooperates with us" (*ST* I-II, q. 111, a. 2, ad 3).

Finally, Aquinas identifies a distinction between *prevenient grace* and *subsequent grace*. This distinction indicates that some graces—prevenient graces—precede other graces, and subsequent graces follow upon those already given. Thus, "the division into prevenient and subsequent grace does not divide grace in its essence, but only in its effect" (*ST* I-II, q. 111, a. 3, ad 2).

The Cause and Effects of Grace (ST *I-II, qq. 112–114)*

Simply speaking, God alone is the cause of grace. It is impossible for any creature to cause grace because "the gift of grace surpasses every capability of created nature, since it is nothing short of a partaking in the Divine Nature" (*ST* I-II, q. 112, a. 1). God imparts grace, and "every preparation in man must be by the help of God moving the soul to good" (*ST* I-II, q. 112, a. 2). "Hence it is said that man's will is prepared by God [for grace], and that man's steps are guided by God" in grace (*ST* I-II, q. 112, a. 2).

Aquinas also observes that not all have an "equal measure" of grace (*ST* I-II, q. 112, a. 4, s.c.). Although all who possess sanctifying grace are truly joined to God, objectively, not all subjectively possess grace to the same degree: "One may be more perfectly enlightened by grace than another" (*ST* I-II, q. 112, a. 4). And because God is the ultimate cause of grace, the "first cause of this diversity [of grace among different people] is to be sought on the part of the God, Who dispenses His gifts of grace variously, in order that the beauty and perfection of the Church may result from these various degree" (*ST* I-II, q. 112, a. 4).

Because grace is supernatural—and, therefore, not susceptible to natural perception or verification—it is only by divine revelation that anyone can know, with absolute certitude, that they possess grace. Nonetheless, the presence of grace can be perceived in someone's life "conjecturally by signs; and thus anyone may know that he has grace, when he is conscious of delighting in God, and of despising worldly things, and inasmuch as a man is not conscious of any mortal sin" (*ST* I-II, q. 113, a. 5).

Aquinas identifies two effects of grace—effects corresponding to the distinction between operating and cooperating grace: "(1) The justification of the ungodly, which is the effect of operating grace; and (2) merit, which is the effect of cooperating grace" (*ST* I-II, q. 113, prol.).

Justification is "the remission of sins" (*ST* I-II, q. 113, a. 1). "The effect of the Divine love in us, which is taken away by sin, is grace, whereby a man is made worthy of eternal life, from which sin shuts him out. Hence we could not conceive the remission of guilt, without the infusion of grace" (*ST* I-II, q. 113, a. 2). Aquinas makes the dramatic observation that "the justification of the ungodly, which terminates at the eternal good of a share in the Godhead, is greater than the creation of heaven and earth, which terminates at the good of mutable nature" (*ST* I-II, q. 113, a. 9).

Merit refers to the fact that the human person can truly cooperate with divine grace. Grace truly informs the being and actions of the human person. Aquinas explains that a meritorious work can be considered in two ways: "first, as it proceeds from free-will; secondly, as it proceeds from the grace of the Holy Spirit" (*ST* I-II, q. 114, a. 3). Moreover, any meritorious work necessarily depends upon the theological virtue of charity (*ST* I-II, q. 114, a. 4).

And it is to the theological virtues that Aquinas devotes his attentions in the *Secunda secundae,* the next part of the *ST*.

II-II. The Second Part of the Second Part: The Virtues

CHAPTER 10

The Theological Virtues

(ST II-II, qq. 1–46)

The *Secunda secundae* addresses moral matters in their particularity. "After a general consideration of virtues, vices, and other things pertaining to moral matters" in the *Prima secundae*, "it is necessary to consider each of them in particular." The reason for this greater particularity lies in the fact that "universal moral discourse is less useful, since actions are singulars" (*ST* II-II, prol.), and "the study of morals . . . treats of human acts" (*ST* I-II, q. 6, prol.).

Aquinas observes that "particular moral matters can be considered in two ways: first, with respect to the moral matter itself, for example, this virtue or that vice; second, with respect to the special states of men, for example subjects and prelates, people in active or contemplative life, and so on for other differences of men." Thus, the *Secunda secundae* firstly considers "in particular everything that pertains to people of whatever state"—virtues and vices. Secondly, it considers "what pertains to people in special states of life" (*ST* II-II, prol.).

Thus, we can outline the *Secunda secundae* in the following manner:

"Moral Matter Itself" (*ST* II-II, qq. 1–170):

- **Theological Virtues (*ST* II-II, qq. 1–46)**
    - Faith (*ST* II-II, qq. 1–16)
    - Hope (*ST* II-II, qq. 17–22)
    - Charity (*ST* II-II, qq. 23–46)
- **Moral Virtues (*ST* II-II, qq. 47–170)**
    - Prudence (*ST* II-II, qq. 47–56)
    - Justice (*ST* II-II, qq. 57–122)

- Fortitude (*ST* II-II, qq. 123–140)
- Temperance (*ST* II-II, qq. 141–170)

"Special States of Life" (*ST* II-II, qq. 171–189)

Order of Teaching and Learning the Virtues

Even when addressing the complexities of the moral life, Aquinas reiterates his ongoing commitment to a precise, systematic, and carefully crafted presentation of sacred doctrine (see chapter 1). "If we were to treat virtues, gifts, vices and commandments separately, we would have to say the same thing many times over." Such repetition would compromise the purpose of the *ST*: to present sacred doctrine in a preeminently ordered manner. "Therefore, it will be briefer and quicker to treat together the virtue and the gift corresponding to [the virtue], along with the opposite vices, and the affirmative and negative commandments" (*ST* II-II, prol.).

Aquinas thus identifies the elements that will shape his presentation of the virtues in the *Secunda secundae*: (1) the specific virtue itself, (2) the corresponding gifts of the Holy Spirit, (3) the vices opposing each virtue, and (4) the commandments related to each virtue.

It may surprise readers that Aquinas frames his presentation of the moral life in the *Secunda secundae* around the virtues rather than around vices and sins. The Christian life is frequently framed as a journey away from sin. Aquinas, certainly, does not downplay the danger of moral disorder. Yet he consistently reminds readers that sin is parasitic in nature. Vices are *privations*—thus, they are only intelligible in relation to virtue and to good human actions. "Virtues act correctly with regard to the same matter as the opposite vices deviate from." We can only understand vicious *disorder* if we first understand virtuous *order*. Therefore, "all moral matters are reduced to the consideration of the virtues" (*ST* II-II, prol.). The perfective order of the virtues maintains absolute priority over the defective disorder of the vices.

The *Secunda secundae* begins with the theological virtues, rather than with the cardinal moral virtues, because the *ST* is a work of sacred doctrine. Although natural reality and human reason are significant in the *ST*, the light of faith and divine grace are of preeminent and shaping importance in sacred theology. God is the object and end of sacred doctrine. God is also the direct object and end of the theological virtues. Therefore, the exposition of the theological virtues precedes that of the cardinal virtues. Indeed, the effects of grace within the cardinal virtues can only be appreciated after the nature and dynamics of the theological virtues have received adequate consideration.

God: The Object of the Theological Virtues

The theological virtues are the effect of sanctifying grace in the soul of the Christian. Sanctifying grace is an entitative habit. This means that grace resides in the essence of the human soul. The human soul, as we have seen in chapter 6, has powers. Sanctifying grace "overflows" into the powers of the soul, qualifying them in a way that reflects their respective natures and actions (*ST* I-II, q. 110, a. 3).

Thus, the distinction between the theological virtues arises from the different powers of the human person in relation to God. God activates the rational powers of the human person in different ways (i.e., according to different objects). "Man in his intellective powers participates in the Divine knowledge through the virtue of faith, and in his power of will participates in the Divine love through the virtue of charity" (*ST* I-II, q. 110, a. 4).

The theological virtues render the powers of the soul able to act in a way that is ordered to God himself. Hence, these virtues are called "theological" for three reasons: (1) "their object is God, inasmuch as they direct us aright to God"; (2) "they are infused in us by God alone"; and (3) "these virtues are not made known to us, save by Divine revelation" (*ST* I-II, q. 62, a. 1).

As we will see at greater length in the following chapter, the moral virtues are ordered to different types of good that characterize the human journey to God. "The intellectual and moral virtues perfect man's intellect and appetite according to the capacity of human nature; the theological virtues, supernaturally" (*ST* I-II, q. 62, a. 2). The theological virtues are supernatural in nature. They perfect the human person with regard to "a happiness surpassing man's nature, and which man can obtain by the power of God alone, by a kind of participation of the Godhead" (*ST* I-II, q. 62, a. 1).

Faith (*ST* II-II, qq. 1–16)

The first question of the *Secunda secundae* examines the *object* of faith. As we noted in previous chapters, objects specify actions and, consequently, habits. The object of faith is of supreme importance for understanding this theological virtue.

God as *First Truth* is the specific object of the theological virtue of faith. As a habit that resides in the intellectual power of the human person, faith is cognitive in nature (*ST* II-II, q. 4, a. 2). Aquinas explains that "the object of every cognitive habit includes two things: first, that which is known materially, and is the material object, so to speak, and, second, that whereby it is known, which is the formal aspect of the object." In order to illustrate his point, Aquinas invokes geometry as an example: "In the science of geometry, the conclusions are what is known materially, while the formal aspect of the science is the mean of demonstration, through which the conclusions are known" (*ST* II-II, q. 1, a. 1). Although the material and the formal objects are both important to any habit, the formal object is of supreme importance. Why? The formal object (or formal "aspect") of a habit specifies precisely *how* material objects are considered.

In the theological virtue of faith, thus, God as First Truth is the "formal aspect of the object." For faith "does not assent to anything except because it is revealed by God. Hence the mean on which faith is based is the Divine Truth" (*ST* II-II, q. 1, a. 1). God as highest, divine, and revealing truth is the formal object of faith. Consequently, "an act of faith is *to believe God* [*credere Deo*]" (*ST* II-II, q. 6, a. 2; italics in the original). In other words, the formal motivation of faith is simply and exclusively the fact that God has revealed it. The light of God's divine revelation is the formal "means" through which faith knows what it knows.

The material object of faith is, principally, truths about God. In this way, the material object of faith can be characterized as "to believe in a God" (*credere Deum*, in Latin)—because "nothing is proposed to our belief, except inasmuch as it is referred to God" himself (*ST* II-II, q. 2, a. 2). Nonetheless, any truth that God reveals is a material object of faith. In addition to truths about God himself, God also reveals "many other things" in reference to himself (*ST* II-II, q. 1, a. 1). Thus, Aquinas explains that "things concerning Christ's human nature, and the sacraments of the Church, or any creatures whatever, come under faith, insofar as by them we are directed to God, and inasmuch as we assent to them on account of the Divine Truth" (*ST* II-II, q. 1, a. 1, ad 1).

We do not believe through theological faith because we naturally "see" the truths of the propositions of faith. Rather, "the light of faith makes us see what we believe" (*ST* II-II, q. 1, a. 2). Belief comes first. Thus, "faith has not that research of natural reason which demonstrates what is believed, but a research into those things whereby a man is induced to believe, for instance that such things have been uttered by God and confirmed by miracles" (*ST* II-II, q. 2, a. 1, ad 1).

*The Act of Faith (*ST *II-II, qq. 2–3)*

The interior act of faith is *to believe*. This act is an act of the intellect. Nonetheless, it is not an act of the intellect alone. Indeed, the precise act of faith is *to believe*—"to think with assent." This movement to intellectual assent arises from the *will*. "The intellect of the believer is determined to one object, not by the reason, but by the will, wherefore assent is taken here for an act of the intellect as determined to one object by the will" (*ST* II-II, q. 2, a. 1, ad 3). Aquinas explains further, "For, since *to believe* is an act of the intellect, insofar as the will moves it to assent . . . the object of faith can be considered either on the part of the intellect, or on the part of the will that moves the intellect" (*ST* II-II, q. 2, a. 2). Insofar as the will moves the intellect to assent to God, "an act of faith is *to believe in God* [*credere in Deum*]. For the First Truth is referred to the will, through having the aspect of the end" (*ST* II-II, q. 2, a. 2).

In sum, Aquinas describes the act of belief in three ways, each related to God as object: (1) God is the formal object of faith—to believe God, *credere Deo*. (2) God is the material object of faith—to believe in a God, *credere Deum*. (3) Because the will moves the intellect to an act of belief, God is also the object of the will—to believe in God, *credere in Deum*.

The confluence of these three elements in the act of faith reveals why the act is meritorious and salvific. "Our actions are meritorious insofar as they proceed from the free-will moved with grace by God." And "the act of believing is an act of the intellect assenting to the Divine truth at the command of the will moved by the grace of God" (*ST* II-II, q. 2, a. 9).

The interior act of faith leads to the exterior act of faith: confession or profession of faith. Although faith resides within the intellect of the human person, this theological virtue is not a completely hidden virtue. The interior act of belief always expresses itself—at the right times and in appropriate ways. "For the outward utterance is intended to signify the inward thought. Wherefore, just as the inward thought of matters of faith is properly an act of faith, so too is the outward confession of them" (*ST* II-II, q. 3, a. 1).

*Theological Faith as a Virtue (*ST *II-II, qq. 4–7)*

As we have seen, faith resides in the intellect (*ST* II-II, q. 4, a. 2). Yet, Aquinas also emphasizes the fact that theological *charity* is the "form of faith." "Charity is called the form of faith because it quickens the act of faith" (*ST* II-II, q. 4, a. 3, ad 1). In other words, "the act of faith is perfected and formed by charity"—and it is "directed to the object of the will, i.e., the good, as to its end." And this end is nothing less than "the Divine Good, the object of charity" (*ST* II-II, q. 4, a. 3).

Consequently, Aquinas points to the real distinction between *living faith* and *dead faith*. Dead (or "lifeless") faith is present in someone who believes intellectually what God reveals but does not volitionally love him through the theological virtue of charity (*ST* II-II, q. 4, a. 4). Thus, "when living faith becomes lifeless, faith is not changed, but its subject [is changed], the soul, which at one time has faith without charity, and at another time, with charity" (*ST* II-II, q. 4, a. 4, ad 4).

With regard to those who "disbelieve" even one truth of the faith, Aquinas explains that "neither living nor lifeless faith remains" in them (*ST* II-II, q. 5, a. 3). He reminds his readers that "the formal object of faith is the First Truth." Consequently, anyone who "does not adhere, as to an infallible and Divine rule, to the teaching of the Church, which proceeds from the First Truth manifested in Holy Writ, has not the habit of faith, but holds that which is of faith otherwise than by faith" (*ST* II-II, q. 5, a. 3). The formal object of faith unifies the virtue such that it is impossible to believe some but not all doctrines of faith. One either believes all that God reveals—because God is First Truth—or one believes nothing that God reveals. Faith is all or nothing.

Those who possess faith have received this theological virtue from God himself. "Faith as regards the assent which is the chief act of faith, is from God moving man inwardly by grace" (*ST* II-II, q. 6, a. 1). This is not to deny that the human will is important in the act of faith. Indeed, "to believe does indeed depend on the will of the believer: but man's will needs to be prepared by God with grace, in order that he may be raised to things which are above his nature" (*ST* II-II, q. 6, a. 1, ad 3). This explains why the effects of faith include *fear* of God and the *purification of the heart*. Those who receive God's divinely revealed truths fear the absence of God in their lives and the consequences that follow this absence. Moreover, those who live by faith are purified from disordered loves by the orientation of their life to the good who is above all: God himself (*ST* II-II, q. 7).

The Corresponding Gifts of the Holy Spirit: Understanding and Knowledge (ST II-II, qq. 8–9)

The *understanding* that is a gift of the Holy Spirit is a "supernatural light" that enables the human person's intellect "to penetrate into the heart of things" beyond their mere external appearances (*ST* II-II, q. 8, a. 1). Although "faith implies merely assent to what is proposed," the gift of understanding "implies a certain perception of the truth" (*ST* II-II, q. 8, a. 5). Thus, "one who has faith can be enlightened in his mind concerning what he has heard; thus it is written (Luke 24:27, 32) that Our Lord opened the scriptures to His disciples, that they might understand them" (*ST* II-II, q. 8, a. 2, s.c.).

The gift of understanding enables the Christian believer to have "a sound grasp of the things that are proposed to be believed." The *gift of knowledge* enables the believer to have "a sure and right judgment on them, so as to discern what is to be believed, from what is not to be believed" (*ST* II-II, q. 9, a. 1). Specifically, the gift of knowledge pertains to judgments concerning what ought to be believed about "human or created things" (*ST* II-II, q. 9, a. 2).

Vices Opposed to the Virtue of Faith (ST II-II, qq. 10–15)

There are three categories of vices contrary to the theological virtue of faith: *unbelief*, *blasphemy*, and *ignorance and dullness of mind*. Unbelief is opposed to faith. Blasphemy is opposed to the confession of faith. Ignorance and dullness of mind are contrary to the gifts of understanding and knowledge (*ST* II-II, q. 10, prol.).

Hope (*ST* II-II, qq. 17–22)

Hope is the theological virtue by which the graced human person hopes "for anything as being possible to us by means of the Divine assistance." Thus, "our hope attains God Himself, on Whose help it leans" (*ST* II-II, q. 17, a. 1). This theological hope (in distinction from the "hope" of the passions) is ordered to "the infinite good, which is proportionate to the power of our divine helper, since it belongs to an infinite power to lead anyone to an infinite good" (*ST* II-II, q. 17, a. 2). Thus, in this theological virtue, we "hope from him for nothing less than Himself."

Aquinas concludes, "The principal object of hope is eternal happiness," the ultimate "enjoyment of God himself." The Christian legitimately can "hope" for other goods, but only "secondarily and as referred to eternal happiness: just as faith regards God principally, and, secondarily, those things which are referred to God" (*ST* II-II, q. 17, a. 2).

God is the object of hope in two ways: (1) as "a good to be obtained finally" (*ST* II-II, q. 17, a. 6, ad 3), and (2) as the helper "through whom one expects to obtain what one hopes for" (*ST* II-II, q. 19, a. 1). Through hope, we "adhere to God, as the source whence we derive perfect goodness, i.e., insofar as, by hope, we trust to the Divine assistance for obtaining happiness"—in other words, we love God for *our own sake* (*ST* II-II, q. 17, a. 6 and a. 8). In this way, hope is distinguished from both faith and charity. "Faith makes us adhere to God, as the source whence we derive the knowledge of truth, since we believe that what God tells us is true." Through charity, we "adhere to God for His own sake" (*ST* II-II, q. 17, a. 6)—"by uniting our affections to Him, so that we live, not for ourselves, but for God" (*ST* II-II, q. 17, a. 6, ad 3).

The theological virtues of hope and charity both reside in the human will. Thus, they are both virtues ordered to goodness through acts of love (*ST* II-II, q. 18, a. 1). They are distinct, however, insofar as charity "adheres to God for his [God's] own sake," while hopes loves God specifically in order to "obtain" him for oneself (*ST* II-II, q. 17, a. 8). "Consequently," Aquinas explains, "hope, like faith, is voided in heaven." The saints in heaven do not have the theological virtues of faith or hope. These virtues are impossible because they see God as he is directly and are united to him—their happiness is no longer something "future, but present" (*ST* II-II, q. 18, a. 2). "Hope implies a certain defect, namely the futurity of happiness, which ceases when happiness is present" (*ST* II-II, q. 19, a. 11).

The Corresponding Gift of the Holy Spirit: Fear (ST II-II, q. 19)

The fear of God is the Holy Spirit's gift that corresponds to the theological virtue of hope. Indeed, "filial fear and hope cling together, and perfect one another" (*ST* II-II, q. 19, a. 9, ad 1).

Aquinas explains that "the proper object of fear is evil" (*ST* II-II, q. 19, a. 5). As we saw in chapter 6, there are two kinds of evil: the evil of punishment or pain and the evil of fault (*ST* I, q. 48, a. 5). Thus, there are two principal kinds of fear: *servile* and *filial fear*. Servile fear is fear with respect to punishment. Filial fear is "fear of committing a fault . . . for it becomes a child to fear offending its father" (*ST* II-II, q. 19, a. 2). Both servile and filial fear are good insofar as they draw us to God.

Nonetheless, only filial fear is "numbered among the seven gifts of the Holy Spirit." The gift of fear renders the human agent "amenable to the motion of the Holy Spirit." Through filial fear, "we revere God and avoid separating ourselves from Him." This fear is foundational to the whole of the Christian life. Thus, Aquinas says, "filial fear holds the first place, as it were, among the gifts of the Holy Spirit, in the ascending order" (*ST* II-II, q. 19, a. 9).

*Vices Opposed to the Virtue of Hope (*ST *II-II, qq. 20–21)*

There are two specific vices contrary to the theological virtue of hope: *despair* and *presumption*. Aquinas explains that despair is so pernicious that it is "not only a sin but also the origin of other sins" (*ST* II-II, q. 20, a. 1). Hence, "despair is a most grievous sin" (*ST* II-II, q. 20, a. 3).

Despair proceeds from a "false opinion": that God "refuses pardon to the repentant sinner, or that He does not turn sinners to Himself by sanctifying grace." Therefore, as the movement of hope reflects the truth about God's goodness and mercy, "so the contrary movement of despair, which is in conformity with false opinion about God, is vicious and sinful" (*ST* II-II, q. 20, a. 1).

The sins of unbelief (against faith) and hatred of God (against charity) are "against God as He is in Himself, while despair is against Him, according as His good is partaken of by us." Thus, considered in themselves, unbelief and divine hatred are sins far graver than despair. Nonetheless, considered in relation to us, "despair is more dangerous, since hope withdraws from evils and induces us to seek for good things, so that when hope is given up, men rush headlong into sin, and are drawn away from good works" (*ST* II-II, q. 20, a. 3).

Aquinas introduces the sin of *presumption* in relation to the sin of despair: "Just as despair consists in aversion from God, so presumption consists in inordinate conversion to Him" (*ST* II-II, q. 21, a. 1, s.c.). In other words, "presumption seems to imply immoderate hope" (*ST* II-II, q. 21, a. 1). The immoderation of presumption, however, "does not denote excessive hope, as though man hoped too much in God;

but through man hoping to obtain from God something unbecoming of Him; which is the same as to hope too little in Him, since it implies a depreciation of His power" (*ST* II-II, q. 21, a. 2, ad 2).

Presumption's disorder can arise from errors about either the power of the human person or about the power of God. Presumption can arise from an overestimation of the power of the human person "if he tends to a good as though it were possible to him, whereas it surpasses his powers." Presumption can also arise from confusion about the power of God if "a man tends to some good as though it were possible by the power and mercy of God, whereas it is not possible, for instance, if a man hope to obtain pardon without repenting, or glory without merits." Aquinas specifies that this second type of presumption is actually "a sin against the Holy Spirit": "by presuming thus a man removes or despises the assistance of the Holy Spirit, whereby he is withdrawn from sin" (*ST* II-II, q. 21, a. 1).

Charity (*ST* II-II, qq. 23–46)

The formal object of charity is *the divine goodness* (*ST* II-II, q. 23, a. 4). Accordingly, charity must reside within the will. Only the will—as a rational power—can be activated by a nonsensible good: "The object of charity is not a sensible good, but the Divine good which is known by the intellect alone. Therefore the subject of charity is not the sensitive, but the intellective appetite, i.e., the will" (*ST* II-II, q. 25, a. 1). Charity is a created, supernatural habit that God imparts to the will, "inclining that power to the act of charity, and causing it to act with ease and pleasure" (*ST* II-II, q. 25, a. 2).

Charity is also the highest of the theological virtues. "Faith and hope attain God indeed insofar as we derive from Him the knowledge of truth [i.e., faith] or the acquisition of good [i.e., hope], whereas charity attains God himself that it may rest in Him, but not that something may accrue to us from Him" (*ST* II-II, q. 23, a. 6). Charity attains God as he is in himself. Neither faith nor hope "touches" God in this same way.

Because the divine goodness is the ultimate end of everything, "charity is included in the definition of every virtue, not as being essentially every virtue, but because every virtue depends on it in a way" (*ST* II-II, q. 23, a. 4, ad 1). Thus, charity is the *form of all the other virtues*. "In morals the form of an act is taken chiefly from the end. The reason of this is that the principle of moral acts is the will, whose object and form, so to speak, are the end." Thus, because charity "directs the acts of all other virtues to the last end, and which, consequently, also gives the form to all other acts of virtue" (*ST* II-II, q. 23, a. 8). Hence, "charity is called the form of the other virtues not as being their exemplar or their essential form, but rather by way of efficient cause, insofar as it sets the form on all" (*ST* II-II, q. 23, a. 8, ad 1).

Thus, Aquinas explains that charity is a *friendship between God and the human person*. The unique characteristic of friendship is *benevolent communication*: the type of love whereby "we love someone as to wish good to him" and communicate this benevolent love to the beloved. "Since there is communication between man and God, inasmuch as He communicates His happiness to us, some kind of friendship must needs be based on this same communication." Citing 1 Corinthians 1:9, "God is faithful: by Whom you are called unto the fellowship of His Son," Aquinas explains that charity is precisely "the love which is based on this communication" (*ST* II-II, q. 23, a. 1).

In sum, "God is the principal object of charity, while our neighbor is loved out of charity for God's sake" (*ST* II-II, q. 23, a. 5). Thus, the "act whereby we love God, and [the act] whereby we love our neighbor" is "specifically the same act" (*ST* II-II, q. 25, a. 1). Charity loves all things because of and in relation to the divine goodness.

The Act of Charity (ST *II-II, qq. 27–33)*

To love is the act of charity. Because charity is a kind of friendship, "it is clear that to love is more proper to charity than to be loved" (*ST* II-II, q. 27, a. 1). The loving act of charity is more than mere passion or sentiment of "goodwill" toward others (*ST* II-II, q. 27, a. 2). To love in charity implies "a certain union with the beloved, which union is not denoted by goodwill" (*ST* II-II, q. 27, a. 2, ad 2). Thus, the virtue of charity actively "tends to God first, and flows on from Him to other things, and in this sense charity loves God immediately, and other things through God" (*ST* II-II, q. 27, a. 5).

Six effects follow upon the principal act of charity—three of which are *internal*, and three *external*. The three internal effects of charity are joy, peace, and mercy; and the three external effects are beneficence, almsdeeds, and fraternal correction.

There is a "twofold" *joy* that arises from charity. First, the joy whereby "we rejoice in the Divine good considered in itself." The second kind of joy is that "whereby we rejoice in the Divine good as participated by us" (*ST* II-II, q. 28, a. 2).

Peace proceeds from a "twofold union." First, peace is "the result of one's own appetites being directed to one object; while the other results from one's own appetite being united with the appetite of another." Charity causes both types of union: "the first, insofar as man loves God with his whole heart, by referring all things to Him, so that all his desires tend to one object—the second, insofar as we love our neighbor as ourselves" (*ST* II-II, q. 29, a. 3).

Mercy refers to the compassion one has for another's misery (*ST* II-II, q. 30, a. 1). "Mercy is accounted as being proper to God," because his omnipotence is "chiefly manifested" through it. In charity, one is merciful insofar as one works to remedy the "defects" a neighbor suffers (*ST* II-II, q. 30, a. 4).

With regard to the three external effects of charity, *beneficence* is the "act of friendship, and, consequently, of charity," whereby someone does good to another (*ST* II-II, q. 31, a. 1). An *almsdeed*, or the act of "giving alms," is a specific kind of beneficence. Aquinas observes with approval that "some have defined alms as being *a deed whereby something is given to the needy, out of compassion for God's sake*" (*ST* II-II, q. 32, a. 1; italics in the original). Almsdeeds touch on both spiritual and bodily needs (*ST* II-II, q. 32, a. 2). Finally, *fraternal correction* is a specific kind of spiritual almsdeed (*ST* II-II, q. 33, a. 1, s.c.). Fraternal correction is charitable insofar as it is aimed at our friend's good.

*Vices Opposed to the Virtue of Charity (*ST *II-II, qq. 34–43) and the Precepts of Charity (*ST *II-II, q. 44)*

Aquinas identifies the sins against charity: "(1) hatred, which is opposed to love; (2) sloth and envy, which are opposed to the joy of charity; (3) discord and schism, which are contrary to peace; (4) offense and scandal, which are contrary to beneficence and fraternal correction" (*ST* II-II, q. 34, prol.). Each sin against charity is a deviation from the loving order of charity and its proper effects. These sins directly contradict the two precepts of charity: to love God and neighbor (*ST* II-II, q. 44). These precepts fittingly summarize the whole of charity because by the first "we are induced to love as our end," and by the other "we are led to love our neighbor for God's sake" (*ST* II-II, q. 44, a. 3).

*The Corresponding Gift of the Holy Spirit: Wisdom (*ST *II-II, qq. 45–46)*

Wisdom is the gift of the Holy Spirit that corresponds to the theological virtue of faith: "It belongs to wisdom to consider the highest cause." Unlike acquired wisdom, which is an intellectual virtue, the gift of wisdom is a supernatural habit received "from above." And unlike the theological virtue of faith, which *assents* to divine truth, the gift of wisdom *judges* according to divine truth (*ST* II-II, q. 45, a. 1). In sum, wisdom is the gift of the Holy Spirit that "enables us to judge aright of Divine things, or of other things according to divine rules, by reason of a certain connaturalness or union with Divine things, which is the effect of charity" (*ST* II-II, q. 45, a. 4). The gift of wisdom is, consequently, both speculative and practical in nature. It is speculative insofar as wisdom "contemplates Divine things in themselves." It is practical "insofar as it judges of human acts by Divine things, and directs human acts according to Divine rules" (*ST* II-II, q. 45, a. 3).

Folly is the vice that opposes the gift of wisdom. Folly "denotes dullness of sense in judging, and chiefly as regards the highest cause, which is the last end and the sovereign good" (*ST* II-II, q. 46, a. 2). This sin "is caused by the spiritual sense being dulled, so as to be incapable of judging spiritual things." Folly "arises chiefly from lust," because "man's sense is plunged into earthly things chiefly by lust, which is the greatest of pleasures; and these absorb the mind more than any others" (*ST* II-II, q. 46, a. 3).

Chapter 11

The Cardinal Virtues

(ST II-II, qq. 47–170)

As noted in the previous chapter, Aquinas's consideration of the moral virtues follows his consideration of the theological virtues. Because the *ST* is a work of sacred theology, and because the theological virtues have God for their object, they have a priority over the moral virtues. Aquinas structures his examination of the moral virtues around the four pivotal (i.e., "cardinal") moral virtues:

- **Cardinal Virtues (*ST* II-II, qq. 47–170)**
  - Prudence (*ST* II-II, qq. 47–56)
  - Justice (*ST* II-II, qq. 57–122)
  - Fortitude (*ST* II-II, qq. 123–140)
  - Temperance (*ST* II-II, qq. 141–170)

The length of the treatises on the moral virtues is not gratuitous. As is the case with everything in the *ST*, each component of Aquinas's presentation of the cardinal virtues is conceived with precision and composed with care. The moral virtues are more *complex* than the theological virtues. Even a cursory examination of the *Secunda secundae*'s different parts confirms this claim. The *ST*'s treatment of the moral virtues is almost three times as long as that of the theological virtues.

The reason for the complexity of the moral virtues is tied to the fact that they are about the *means* to our end (i.e., beatific goodness, God himself). And these means—as contingent realities—are variegated and contingent. Human life has many elements and parts. And the human journey to God must navigate through the complexity of human contingency. Therefore, the moral virtues are intrinsically complex in a way completely foreign to the simplicity of the theological virtues (which concern God, our supernatural end).

It would be impossible in a book of this size to summarize the moral virtues—both acquired and infused—to an exhaustive degree. Here as elsewhere, no other reading can replace or displace that of reading the *ST* directly. Thus, the following pages are only meant to provide a concise overview of some of the key elements of the moral virtues in their particularity.

To aid our survey of these virtues, we can consult the following diagram that helpfully depicts the broad features of each of the theological and the moral virtues. This diagram outlines the unity among and the distinctions between the different virtues we have explored thus far and the virtues that we will examine in the next several pages.[1]

A Summary of the Moral Virtues

Aquinas gives us a helpful summary of the moral virtues:

> Hence human virtue, of which we are speaking now, is that which makes a man good, and tenders his work good. Now man's good is to be in accordance with reason. . . . Wherefore it belongs to human virtue to make man good, to make his work accord with reason. This happens in three ways: first, by rectifying reason itself, and this is done by the intellectual virtues; secondly, by establishing the rectitude of reason in human affairs, and this belongs to justice; thirdly, by removing the obstacles to the establishment of this rectitude in human affairs. Now the human will is hindered in two ways from following the rectitude of reason. First, through being drawn by some object of pleasure to something other than what the rectitude of reason requires; and this obstacle is removed by the virtue of temperance. Secondly, through the will being disinclined to follow that which is in accordance with reason, on account of some difficulty that presents itself. In order to remove this obstacle fortitude of the mind is requisite, whereby to resist the aforesaid difficulty even as a man, by fortitude of body, overcomes and removes bodily obstacles. (*ST* II-II, q. 123, a. 1)

The first thing that Aquinas reminds us of is the essence of virtue: virtue is that which makes both an actor and his or her action *good*. Virtue is

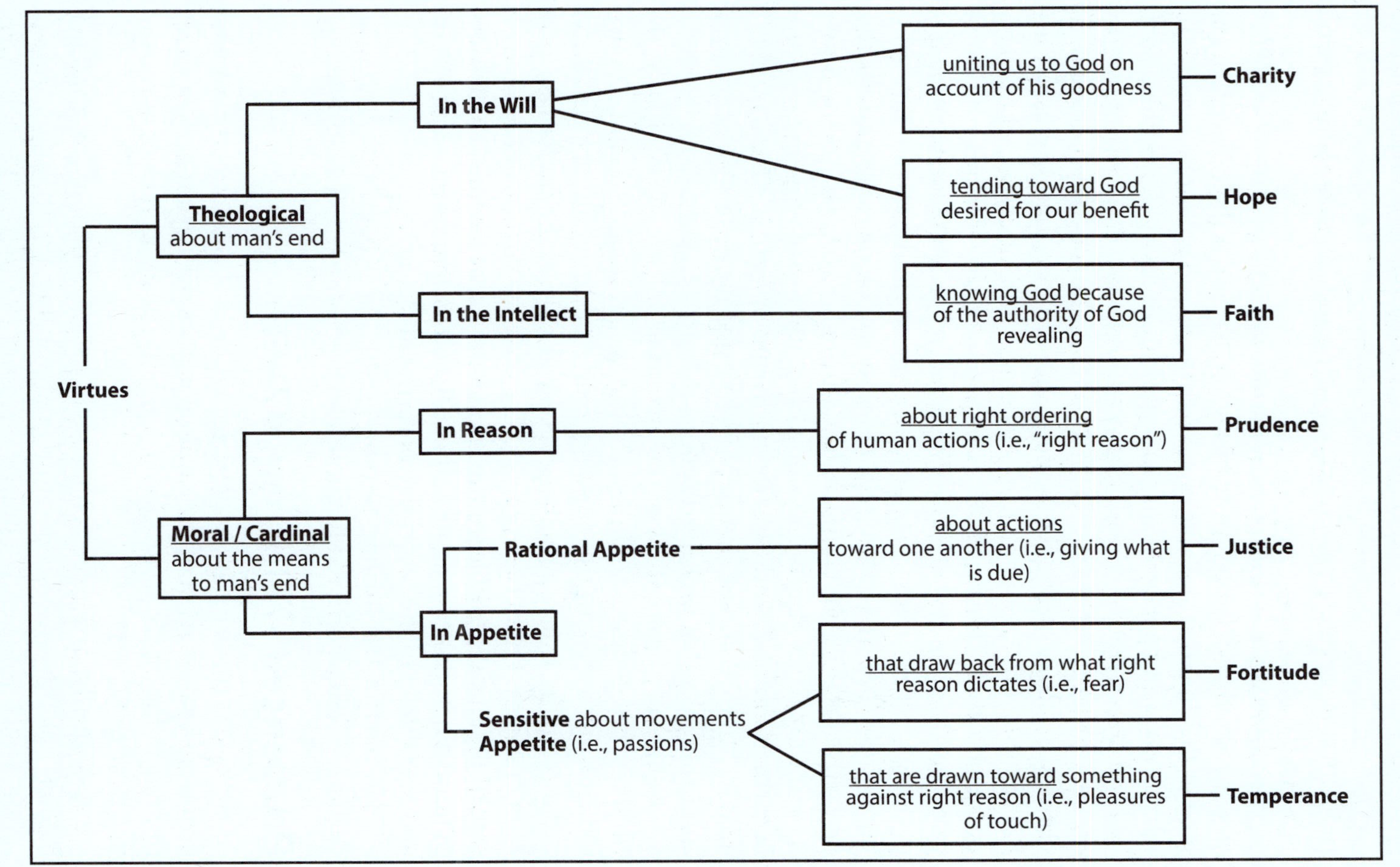
Virtues
Theological
about man's end
In the Will
uniting us to God on
account of his goodness
Charity
tending toward God
desired for our benefit
Hope
In the Intellect
knowing God because
of the authority of God
revealing
Faith
Moral / Cardinal
about the means
to man's end
In Reason
about right ordering
of human actions (i.e., "right reason")
Prudence
In Appetite
Rational Appetite
about actions
toward one another (i.e., giving what
is due)
Justice
Sensitive about movements
Appetite (i.e., passions)
that draw back from what right
reason dictates (i.e., fear)
Fortitude
that are drawn toward something
against right reason (i.e., pleasures
of touch)
Temperance

perfective. It is perfective of us in our being and in our activities. Virtue is perfective ordering.

Because virtue is perfective in nature, the inherent order of perfection is something recognizable by *reason*. Reason is the power that can look at the "big picture" of human existence and activity—identifying what is good and perfective of our nature and activity (as well as what is bad and defective vis-à-vis our nature and activity). Thus, virtue requires the well-ordering of reason itself. This requirement corresponds to the virtue of *prudence*. Secondly, the perfective ordering of right reason must be *established* in human affairs. This establishment corresponds to the virtue of *justice*. Thirdly, all *impediments* to this establishment must be removed. The removal of those things that impede the establishment of perfective order in human affairs corresponds to the virtues located in the *sensitive appetites*. Precisely, the virtue of *temperance* ensures that perfective order is not compromised through feelings of "being drawn by some object of pleasure to something other than what the rectitude of virtue requires." Additionally, the virtue of *fortitude* (or "courage") ensures that we do not shrink before perfective order "on account of some difficulty that presents itself."

Aquinas's presentation of the virtues is holistic. It recognizes the fundamental goodness of human nature as irrevocably inclined to that which is perfective of the human person. Additionally, the perfective order of virtue is not something reserved only to the highest parts of human nature. Quite the contrary. The order of virtuous flourishing is something that is possible for the human person as a whole. Each aspect of human nature—the intellect, the will, and the emotions—can receive and participate in the perfective ordering of virtue.

No part of the human person is outside of God's providential designs—designs ordered to goodness, flourishing, and beatitude.

Prudence (*ST* II-II, qq. 47–56)

As we have seen, virtue is about perfective order. Consequently, Aquinas begins his examination of the cardinal virtues with prudence—a virtue residing in the *intellect*. "Prudence, properly speaking, resides in reason" (*ST* II-II, q. 47, a. 1).[2]

Specifically, prudence is a virtue of *practical reason*: "to prudence belongs not only the consideration of reason, but also the application to action, which is the end of practical reason" (*ST* II-II, q. 47, a. 3). All of this culminates in this virtue's traditional definition: "prudence is right reason applied to action" (*ST* II-II, q. 47, a. 2, s.c.). The specific object of the virtue of prudence, thus, is something that can be done, "that is, with things that have their being in the doer himself" (*ST* II-II, q. 47, a. 5). Prudence, therefore, is about human actions—those actions that flow from the inherent depths of the human person as a rational actor.

The precise definition and specific object of prudence point toward the centrality of this virtue in the Christian life. In other words, prudence is not an isolated virtue. The perfective ordering of prudence extends to all of human life and activity—all of those "means" ordered to the perfective end of the human person (*ST* II-II, q. 47, a. 6). "The proper end of each moral virtue consists precisely in conformity with right reason." Thus, "it belongs to prudence to decide in what manner and by what means man shall obtain the mean of reason in his deeds" (*ST* II-II, q. 47, a. 7). Without exaggeration, all concrete enactments of the other virtues—including the theological virtues!—depend upon prudence.

It is important to emphasize, however, that prudence is not a "one-size-fits-all" virtue. Prudence is always ordered to human flourishing, but the concrete and particular shape of such flourishing is not necessarily identical for all people at all times (*ST* II-II, q. 47, a. 7, ad 3). For example, it could be reasonable for a professional athlete to attempt to lift heavy weights in the gym while, simultaneously, being unreasonable for an elderly man or woman to do so. Prudential reasoning considers the whole of the situation.

Although prudence resides in human reason, it is not quarantined to the intellect. This virtue does not terminate in an act of knowledge only but rather in the actual execution (or "command") of virtuous action (*ST* II-II, q. 47, a. 8). No one is prudent merely by recognizing or planning perfective order. No one can be prudent in theory only. Real prudence requires the *enactment* of virtue in our actions.

Aquinas then proceeds to examine the different "parts" of prudence (*ST* II-II, q. 48). These parts constitute the different elements and contexts of this virtue. The *integral parts* of prudence are those "things which need to concur for the perfect act of virtue" (*ST* II-II, q. 48, a. 1). Examples of these constitutive elements include *reasoning*, *foresight*, *circumspection*, and *caution*.

Prudential (right) reason about human action takes account of different contexts of human life and activity. These contexts account for the different *subjective parts* of virtue: "the prudence whereby a man rules himself" (i.e., "monastic prudence") differs specifically from "the prudence whereby a man governs a multitude" (e.g., in the case of a family, a city, or an army) (*ST* II-II, q. 48, a. 1).

Finally, there are virtues "which are connected with prudence"—virtues that aid and assist the steps requisite for the virtue of prudence. These virtues (or *potential parts* of prudence) aid the prudent person in the necessary steps of receiving wise *counsel* and formulating a sound *judgment* about what should be done in a given situation.

The Gift of Counsel

Because human life is complex—and complex even for the prudent man or woman—God does not shy away from directly aiding us in our prudential judgments. He offers this aid through the gift of the Holy Spirit known as the *gift of counsel*.

Aquinas reminds us that the gifts of the Holy Spirit "are dispositions whereby the soul is rendered amenable to the motion of the Holy [Spirit]" (*ST* II-II, q. 52, a. 1). Because God moves all creatures according to their natures—according to what they are—he moves the human person in a rational way. "It is proper to the rational creature to be moved through the research of reason [*inquisitio rationis*] to perform any particular action, and this research [*inquisitio*] is called counsel" (*ST* II-II, q. 52, a. 1).

Because "prudence, which denotes rectitude of reason, is chiefly perfected and helped through being ruled and moved by the Holy [Spirit], and this belongs to the gift of counsel. . . . Therefore the gift of counsel corresponds to prudence, as helping and perfecting it" (*ST* II-II, q. 52, a. 2).

Justice (*ST* II-II, qq. 57–122)

The virtue of justice is defined as "rendering to each one his right"—to that which is due to another (*ST* II-II, q. 58, a. 1). Hence, this virtue is about how human persons relate to someone else precisely *as other* (*ST* II-II, q. 58, a. 2). The virtue of justice resides in the *rational appetite* because it is the appetite that follows reason—and reason is able to perceive the order that exists between persons. The virtue of justice shapes, orders, and perfects the operations of the *will*. The will, thus, is the *subject* of the virtue of justice (*ST* II-II, q. 58, a. 4).

Justice presupposes three elements: (1) *A plurality of persons*. And this plurality must comprise at least two persons, but it may comprise more. (2) *A specific kind of relationality among the plurality of persons*: A relationality of *alterity*—the other as other. The relation of justice is not *immediate* but is a relation *mediated* by a particular thing (the "right," or *ius* in Latin). What is owed to the other. (3) Justice requires one relate to another *not* to the other in himself but to *the other as having a right*—indeed, as having a particular right or claim. And such claims are *real*—things and relations really owed to another.

There are different kinds of "rights." *Natural rights*: Those things that belong to a human person due to the fact that they are a human person. This is the fundamental right and is grounded in the natural law. *Positive rights*: Because human nature inclines us to live in society, there are other rights that emerge from humans as living in society. Positive rights are the *conventions* (developed by reason and will) that facilitate an ordered society. *Law of the nations* (*ius gentium*): This is the right that resides between the natural and the positive. It comprises the *natural ordering* of the human person and the *human institutions and conventions* that follow from the circumstantial setting of this natural ordering.

In order to further elucidate the distinct formality of justice, Aquinas contrasts this virtue with the virtues of the sensitive appetites. Temperance and fortitude are considered with the proper ordering (i.e., "the mean") of the passions. And this proper order is discovered through an investigation into *the human person in whom the passions reside*—individually. "Hence the mean in such like virtues is measured not by the proportion of one thing to another, but merely by comparison with the virtuous man himself, so that with them the mean is only that which is fixed by reason in our regard." In contrast, "the matter of justice is external operation, in so far as an operation or the thing used in that operation is duly proportionate to another person." Consequently, Aquinas concludes that justice observes a "real mean"—a *real* order existing between persons (*ST* II-II, q. 58, a. 10).

Consequently, a precise and accurate *restitution* is required in cases of injustice because "it re-establishes equality" (*ST* II-II, q. 64, a. 4, s.c.). Admittedly, an act of restitution is not always easy even if it is required. Aquinas helps his readers to determine how one ought to make restitution in cases where the precise way to make such restitution is unclear:

> If the person to whom restitution is due is unknown altogether, restitution must be made as far as possible, for instance by giving an alms for his spiritual welfare (whether he be dead or living): but not without previously making a careful inquiry about his person. If the person to whom restitution is due be dead, restitution should be made to his heir, who is looked upon as one with him. If he be very far away, what is due to him should be sent to him, especially if it be of great value and can easily be sent: else it should be deposited in a safe place to be kept for him, and the owner should be advised of the fact. (*ST* II-II, q. 62, a. 5, ad 3)

Aquinas also explains that there are different types of justice. *Legal justice* is ordered to the common good. This type of justice regulates the obligations that members of the political community have toward the common good of the community. *Particular justice* is ordered to the good of another individual human person. Its proper activity is to render to each what is proper to each (*ST* II-II, q. 58, a. 9, ad 3). Particular justice can also be further divided into *commutative justice* and *distributive justice* (*ST* I, q. 61, a. 1). Distributive justice regulates what individuals particularly *receive* (i.e., distribution) from the common good. It protects the rights that a member has as part of a specific community. Commutative justice regulates the *exchanges* that occur between individuals. It protects the rights of one person in relation to another. Aquinas explains that "distributive and commutative justice differ not only in respect of unity and multitude, but also in respect of different kinds of due: because common property is due to an individual in one way, and his personal property in another way" (*ST* II-II, q. 61, a. 1, ad 3). Consequently, we can recognize that "equality is the general form of justice." With respect to the formality of equality, commutative and distributive justice agree. They differ insofar as "in one we find equality of geometrical proportion [i.e., distributive justice], whereas in the other we find equality of arithmetical proportion [i.e., commutative justice]" (*ST* II-II, q. 61, a. 2, ad 2).

Because justice is about the real mean that exists between persons, this virtue is concerned with "external things, not by making them, which pertains to art, but by using them in our dealings with other men" (*ST* II-II, q. 58, a. 3, ad 3). This virtue is extremely important for human life because of its proximity to truth: "Since the will is the rational appetite, when the rectitude of the reason which is called truth is imprinted on the will on account of its nighness to the reason, this imprint retains the name of truth; and hence it is that justice sometimes goes by the name of truth" (*ST* II-II, q. 58, a. 4, ad 1).

The Gift of Piety

Piety is the gift of the Holy Spirit that corresponds to the virtue of justice. Piety is associated with the duty and honor that one pays to one's physical father. "The piety that is a gift pays this to God as Father" (*ST* II-II, q. 121, a. 1, ad 1). Through the gift of piety, the Holy Spirit "moves us to this effect among others, of having filial affection towards God, according to Rm. 8:15, 'You have received the spirit of adoption of sons, whereby we cry: Abba (Father)'" (*ST* II-II, q. 121, a. 1). The beatitude "blessed are the meek" is also associated with this gift of the Holy Spirit because of the consonance between meekness and piety (*ST* II-II, q. 121, a. 2).

Fortitude (*ST* II-II, qq. 123–140)

Aquinas explains that "the term 'fortitude' [sometimes translated as 'courage'] can be taken in two ways. First, as simply denoting a certain firmness of mind." Consequently, "in this sense it is a general virtue, or rather a condition of every virtue." But "fortitude" can also "be taken to denote firmness only in bearing and withstanding those things wherein it is most difficult to be firm, namely in certain grave dangers" (*ST* II-II, q. 123, a. 2). It is in this second sense that fortitude is a distinct moral virtue.

"Fortitude is directed to evils of the body, as contraries which it withstands, and to the good of reason, as the end, which it intends to safeguard" (*ST* II-II, q. 123, a. 11, ad 2). The moral virtue of fortitude applies the order that the virtue of prudence recognizes to the *irascible sensitive appetite*. We recall that the object of the irascible appetite is "an arduous or difficult" good or evil (*ST* I-II, q. 23, a. 1). Thus, "fortitude is chiefly about fear of difficult things, which can withdraw the will from following the reason." This virtue enables us to act in a perfective, well-ordered manner even when facing grave threats. Fortitude enables us "firmly to bear the assault of these difficulties by restraining fear, but also moderately to withstand them, when, to wit, it is necessary to dispel them altogether in order to free oneself therefrom for the future, which seems to come under the notion of daring. Therefore fortitude is about fear and daring, as curbing fear and moderating daring" (*ST* II-II, q. 123, a. 3).

Aquinas does not leave ambiguous the ultimate object of fear: *death.* "It belongs to the virtue of fortitude to guard the will against being withdrawn from the good of reason through fear of bodily evil. . . . Hence fortitude of soul must be that which binds the will firmly to the good of reason in the face of the greatest evils." Death is the greatest of all bodily evils "since it does away with all bodily goods." Therefore, Aquinas concludes, "the virtue of fortitude is about the fear of dangers of death" (*ST* II-II, q. 123, a. 4). Lest this sound extreme, Aquinas defends the logic of this conclusion: "Fortitude behaves well in bearing all manner of adversity: yet a man is not reckoned brave simply through bearing any kind of adversity, but only through bearing well even the greatest evils; while through bearing others he is said to be brave in a restricted sense" (*ST* II-II, q. 123, a. 4, ad 1). Thus, one can be courageous (or "fortitudinous") in the face of evils less grave than death, but the greatest of all natural evils (i.e., death) is the ultimate reference point for the virtue of fortitude in its fullest sense.

The dynamics of courage in the face of physical death account for why Aquinas associates the act of *martyrdom* with this virtue (*ST* II-II, q. 124, a. 2). Martyrdom is the act whereby "a man suffer[s] death for Christ's sake" (*ST* II-II, q. 124, a. 4). Aquinas observes that "charity inclines one to the act of martyrdom, as its first and chief motive cause, being the virtue commanding it." Yet fortitude, itself, is the virtue that elicits an act of martyrdom (*ST* II-II, q. 124, a. 2, ad 2).

The Gift of Fortitude

The gift of the Holy Spirit associated with the virtue of fortitude shares its name. Through this gift, the Holy Spirit moves the human soul (or "mind") "in order that he may attain the end of each work begun, and avoid whatever perils may threaten. This surpasses human nature: for sometimes it is not in a man's power to attain the end of his work, or to avoid evils or dangers, since these may happen to overwhelm him in death." Consequently, the Holy Spirit "works this in man, by bringing him to everlasting life, which is the end of all good deeds, and the release from all perils" (*ST* II-II, q. 139, a. 1). The Holy Spirit imparts an infused confidence which expels the fear of "all dangers" (*ST* II-II, q. 139, a. 1, ad 1). "Fortitude, as a virtue, perfects the mind in the endurance of all perils whatever; but it does not go so far as to give confidence of overcoming all dangers: this belongs to the fortitude that is a gift of the Holy [Spirit]" (*ST* II-II, q. 139, a. 1, ad 1). And this gift is associated with the beatitude: "blessed are they that hunger and thirst after righteousness" (*ST* II-II, q. 139, a. 2).

Temperance (*ST* II-II, qq. 141–170)

Temperance is the moral virtue that orders and perfects the operations of the *concupiscible appetite*. We recall that the object of this appetite is "sensible good or evil, simply apprehended as such, which causes pleasure or pain" (*ST* I-II, q. 23, a. 1). This is the appetite that is naturally ordered to the pleasures of food, drink, and sex.

Aquinas reminds his readers that "human virtue is that which inclines man to something in accordance with reason." Temperance is such a virtue because it "moderates" our engagement with sensible goods and pleasures (*ST* II-II, q. 141, a. 1). Sensible goods are not objectively evil, of course. Nonetheless, the human person must enjoy sensible goods in a way that is prudent—in a way that is in accord with the full good of the human person. In this section of the *ST* Aquinas again emphasizes the importance of prudence in relation to all the virtues: "the temperance which fulfills the conditions of perfect virtue is not without prudence" (*ST* II-II, q. 141, a. 1, ad 2). He explains why: "Since, however, man as such is a rational being, it follows that those pleasures are becoming to man which are in accordance with reason. From such pleasures temperance does not withdraw him, but from those which are contrary to reason" (*ST* II-II, q. 141, a. 1, ad 1). The virtue of temperance ensures that human persons avoid any disordered—irrational—engagement with pleasure.

This virtue is very important for human life in general and for the Christian life in particular. "Man's appetite is corrupted chiefly by those things which seduce him into forsaking the rule of reason and Divine law" (*ST* II-II, q. 141, a. 2, ad 1). Because the human person is naturally—and wonderfully!—inclined to that which is good, and sensible goods are the most immediately evident goods, it is easy to find ourselves pursuing these most evident of goods. The right reason of the virtue of prudence is required in order for us to act temperately—to know what kinds, how much, and how frequently sensible goods should be enjoyed.

Hence, temperance safeguards "the good of reason against the passions that rebel against reason" (*ST* II-II, q. 141, a. 3).

And such sensible pleasures are, by definition, the *pleasures of touch*. This is why temperance is "properly about pleasures of meat and drink and sexual pleasures" (*ST* II-II, q. 141, a. 4). Food, drink, and sex are all good things. Nonetheless, not all instances of food, drink, and sexual congress perfect the human person and society. "All the pleasurable objects that are at man's disposal, are directed to some necessity of this life as to their end. Wherefore temperance takes the need of this life, as the rule of the pleasurable objects of which it makes use, and uses them only for as much as the need of this life requires" (*ST* II-II, q. 141, a. 6).

It is important to note that while it is possible to pursue pleasurable things beyond the order recognized by right reason, it is also possible to avoid pleasure to a degree that is also against right reason. In other words, it is possible to have too much *and* too little of pleasures of touch in one's life. "Accordingly, if anyone were to reject pleasure to the extent of omitting things that are necessary for nature's preservation, he would sin, as acting counter to the order of nature. And this pertains to the vice of insensibility" (*ST* II-II, q. 142, a. 1).

The Gift of Fear

The gift of the Holy Spirit that corresponds, "in a manner," to the virtue of temperance is the gift of fear: "whereby a man is withheld from the pleasures of the flesh. . . . The gift of fear has for its principal object God, Whom it avoids offending" (*ST* II-II, q. 141, a. 1, ad 3). While, properly speaking, the virtue of temperance restrains us from disordered pleasures "for the sake of the good appointed by reason," the gift of fear withdraws us from such pleasures "through fear of God" (*ST* I-II, q. 68, a. 4).

Chapter 12

Particularities in Grace and Life

(ST II-II, qq. 171–189)

The *Secunda secundae* concludes with a consideration of differences that characterize human persons under the influence of grace. "After treating individually of all the virtues and vices that pertain to men of all conditions and estates, we must now consider those things which pertain especially to certain men" (*ST* II-II, q. 171, prol.). Although everyone must pursue a life of virtue, not all human persons receive the same kinds of graces, nor do all belong to the same state of life.

Aquinas identifies "a triple difference between men as regards things connected with the soul's habits and acts." The first difference consists in those things related to *gratuitous graces*; the second, the distinction between the *active and the contemplative life*; and the third, the "various duties and states of life" (*ST* II-II, q. 171, prol.).

Differences of Gratuitous Grace (*ST* II-II, qq. 171–178)

We recall from chapter 9 that "gratuitous" refers to those graces ordered to the sanctification of others (not the self). These are expressions of the working of the Holy Spirit, who "provides sufficiently for the Church in matters profitable unto salvation" (*ST* II-II, q. 178, a. 1). There are different gratuitous graces that correspond to *knowledge*, *speech*, and *operation*. We can outline the gratuitous graces, or "gifts," in the following manner:

- **Gratuitous graces of *knowledge*:**
    - Prophecy (*ST* II-II, qq. 171–174)
    - Rapture (*ST* II-II, qq. 175)
- **Gratuitous graces of *speech*:**
    - Tongues (*ST* II-II, q. 176)
    - Words (*ST* II-II, q. 177)
- **Gratuitous grace of *operation*:**
    - Miracles (*ST* II-II, q. 178)

*Gratuitous Graces of Knowledge (*ST *II-II, qq. 171–175)*

Aquinas explains that "all things pertaining to knowledge may be comprised under prophecy, since prophetic revelation extends not only to future events relating to man, but also to things relating to God, both as to those which are to be believed by all and are matters of faith, and as to yet higher mysteries, which concern the perfect and belong to wisdom" (*ST* II-II, q. 171, prol.). Specifically, "the object of prophecy is something known by God and surpassing the faculty of man" (*ST* II-II, q. 174, a. 1).

It is critical to recognize that prophecy extends to more things than merely future events. "Prophets know things that are far [*procul*] removed from man's knowledge" (*ST* II-II, q. 171, a. 1). Thus, "the more remote things are from our knowledge the more pertinent they are to prophecy" (*ST* II-II, q. 171, a. 3). Prophetic knowledge is unique insofar as it "comes through a Divine light, whereby it is possible to know all things both Divine and human, both spiritual and corporeal." Consequently, "prophetic revelation extends" to matters beyond future events (*ST* II-II, q. 171, a. 3).

Prophecy does not arise from the order of nature. "It is requisite to prophecy that the intention of the mind be raised to the perception of Divine things" (*ST* II-II, q. 171, a. 1, ad 4). "Prophetic knowledge is bestowed by Divine enlightenment and revelation." Specifically, the angels serve as "instruments" that convey prophetic knowledge to prophets (*ST* II-II, q. 172, a. 2).

Prophecy is not a habit, however. A habit is a stable disposition in a power, and the grace of prophecy is not stable. "The prophetic light is in the prophet's soul by way of a passion or transitory impression" (*ST* II-II, q. 171, a. 2).

Rapture is the gratuitous grace "whereby a man is uplifted by the spirit of God to things supernatural" (*ST* II-II, q. 175, a. 1). It is a kind of violent ecstasy: "Ecstasy means simply a going out of oneself by being placed outside one's proper order; while rapture denotes a certain violence in addition" (*ST* II-II, q. 175, a. 2, ad 1). The violence of rapture resides in the fact that the *mode* "whereby a man is uplifted to divine things and withdrawn from his senses, is not natural to man" (*ST* II-II, q. 175, a. 1). Nonetheless, Aquinas explains that someone in a state of rapture—St. Paul, for example—may not be separated from the body, yet his intellect was certainly "withdrawn" from "the perception of sensible objects" (*ST* II-II, q. 175, a. 5).

*Gratuitous Graces of Speech (*ST *II-II, qq. 176–177)*

The gratuitous grace of *tongues* refers to the ability to speak in all languages (*ST* II-II, q. 176, a. 1, ad 2). Aquinas associates this grace with "Christ's first disciples," who "were chosen by Him in order that they might disperse throughout the whole world, and preach His faith everywhere, according to Matthew 28:19, Going . . . teach ye all nations" (*ST* II-II, q. 176, a. 1). Aquinas explains that although the Holy Spirit is received even now, "no one speaks in the tongues of all nations, because the Church herself already speaks the languages of all nations" (*ST* II-II, q. 176, a. 1).

By the grace of *words*, "a man not only speaks so as to be understood by different people, which pertains to the gift of tongues, but also speaks with effect" (*ST* II-II, q. 177, a. 1). Through the grace of the word, "the Holy Spirit makes use of the human tongue as an instrument" to (1) instruct the intellect, (2) move the affections, and (3) "sway listeners" to love the realities described by the word (*ST* II-II, q. 177, a. 1).

*Gratuitous Grace of Operation (Miracles) (*ST *II-II, q. 178)*

The grace of miracle working is linked to the grace of tongues and the grace of the word: "Just as the knowledge which a man receives from God needs to be brought to the knowledge of others through the gift of tongues and the grace of the word, so too the word uttered needs to be confirmed in order that it be rendered credible." This confirmation of credibility is accomplished by the working of miracles (*ST* II-II, q. 178, a. 1). "Just as prophecy extends to whatever can be known supernaturally, so the working of miracles extends to all things that can be done supernaturally" (*ST* II-II, q. 178, a. 1, ad 1). Hence, "true miracles" can only occur "by the power of God." And God performs miracles "for man's benefit, and this in two ways: in one way for the confirmation of truth declared, in another way in proof of a person's holiness, which God desires to propose as an example of virtue" (*ST* II-II, q. 178, a. 2).

Differences of Life: Contemplative and Active (*ST* II-II, qq. 179–182)

The distinction between the contemplative and the active life lies in the fact that "certain men are especially intent on the contemplation of truth, while others are especially intent on external actions" (*ST* II-II, q. 179, a. 1). As a Dominican priest, St. Thomas Aquinas himself lived the *contemplative life*. He was personally consecrated to the "contemplation of divine truth."

Although "this contemplation is the end of the whole [of] human life," it "belongs principally to the contemplative life." The contemplation of divine truth will only be perfect in heaven, "when we shall see God face to face." Nonetheless, the contemplative life here on earth "bestows on us a certain inchoate beatitude, which begins now and will be continued in the life to come" (*ST* II-II, q. 180, a. 4).

Aquinas is emphatic that the contemplative life is not a cold, rationalistic, or heartless manner of existence. It is true that "the contemplative life consists chiefly in an act of the intellect." But it "has its beginning in the appetite, since it is through charity that one is urged to the contemplation of God." Hence, "the ultimate perfection of the contemplative life" is divine truth "not only seen but also loved" (*ST* II-II, q. 180, a. 7, ad 1).

Because moral virtues shape and perfect human operation, they "belong essentially" to the occupations of the *active life* (*ST* II-II, q. 181, a. 1). "The active life is more directly concerned with the love of our neighbor," while the "contemplative life pertains directly and immediately to the love of God" (*ST* II-II, q. 182, a. 2). In itself, "the contemplative life is more excellent than the active." Why? "The contemplative life becomes man according to that which is best in him, namely the intellect, and according to its proper objects, namely things intelligible; whereas the active life is occupied with externals." Moreover, "the contemplative life is according to Divine things, whereas active life is according to human things." The "works of the active life" concern "the lower powers [of the human person] also, which are common to us and brutes." Nonetheless, Aquinas recognizes that "in a restricted sense and in a particular case one should prefer the active life on account of the needs of the present life" (*ST* II-II, q. 182, a. 1).

The salvific key for both the contemplative and the active life, however, is charity. It is possible to become a saint through either the contemplative or the active life (*ST* II-II, q. 182, a. 2).

Differences of States of Life (*ST* II-II, qq. 183–189)

Aquinas distinguishes between the different states in life in relation to degrees of "freedom or servitude whether in spiritual or in civil matters" (*ST* II-II, q. 183, a. 1). Within the Church, differences in "states or duties" are ordered to (1) the "perfection of the Church," (2) the "need of those actions which are necessary in the Church," and (3) the order that characterizes the "dignity and beauty of the Church." These differences do not compromise the fundamental unity of the Church as they result "from the unity of faith, charity, and mutual service" (*ST* II-II, q. 183, a. 2).

The perfection of the Christian life "consists radically in charity." The reason for charity's preeminence is not difficult to recognize. "A thing is said to be perfect insofar as it attains its proper end"—and the proper end of the Christian life is God (*ST* II-II, q. 184, a. 1). Thus, "the perfection of charity is paramount in relation to the perfection that regards the other virtues" (*ST* II-II, q. 184, a. 1, ad 2). Of course, perfection considered from "the part of the lover, so that the affective faculty always actually tends to God as much as it possibly can," is not possible in this life. A constant state of continually, actually tending to God is proper to the saints in heaven (*ST* II-II, q. 184, a. 2).

Nonetheless, perfection considered "on the part of the lover as regards the removal of obstacles to the movement of love towards God" is possible in this life. This type of perfection has two expressions in this life. The first type of removal consists in the avoidance of all mortal sins. Because mortal sin is directly opposed to charity, this type of perfection is not exclusive to a specific group of Christians: "It is necessary for salvation." The second seeks to remove from "man's affections not only of whatever is contrary to charity, but also of whatever hinders the mind's affections from tending wholly to God" (*ST* II-II, q. 184, a. 2).

Consequently, "one is said to be in the state of perfection, not through having the act of perfect love, but through binding himself in perpetuity and with a certain solemnity to those things that pertain to perfection" (*ST* II-II, q. 184, a. 4). Aquinas is clear: "those who enter the state of perfection do not profess to be perfect" themselves, but rather "to tend to perfection" (*ST* II-II, q. 184, a. 5, ad 2). Consecrated religious and bishops, or "prelates," are those in this state of perfection. "For religious bind themselves by vow to refrain from worldly affairs, which they might lawfully use, in order more freely to give themselves to God." And "in like manner bishops bind themselves to things pertaining to perfection when they take up the pastoral duty, to which it belongs that a shepherd *lay down his life for his sheep*" (*ST* II-II, q. 184, a. 5; italics in the original).

Specifically, "bishops are in the position of *perfecters*; whereas religious are in the position of being *perfected*" (*ST* II-II, q. 184, a. 7; italics in the original). This is why Aquinas concludes the *Secunda pars* with an examination of the episcopal state (*ST* II-II, q. 185) and the religious state (*ST* II-II, qq. 186–189). Aquinas's closing words reflect how precious he considered his religious vocation to be: "To those indeed who take this sweet yoke [of consecrated life] upon themselves He [Jesus] promises the refreshment of the divine fruition and the eternal rest of their souls. To which may He Who made this promise bring us, Jesus Christ our Lord, *Who is over all things God blessed for ever. Amen*" (*ST* II-II, q. 189, a. 10, ad 3; italics in the original).

III. The Third Part: Jesus Christ and the Sacraments

Chapter 13

Jesus Christ: Our Savior

(ST III, qq. 1–59)

In the prologue to the *Tertia pars*, Aquinas explains that "it is necessary, in order to complete the work of theology, that after considering the last end of human life, and the virtues and vices, there should follow the consideration of the Savior of all, and of the benefits bestowed by Him on the human race" (*ST* III, prol.).

Aquinas divides his examination of Jesus himself into two main parts:

- The mystery of the Incarnation (*ST* III, qq. 1–26)
- The things that Jesus did and suffered (*ST* III, qq. 27–59)

The Mystery of the Incarnation (*ST* III, qq. 1–26)

"Three things occur to be considered" about the mystery of the Incarnation: (1) "the fitness of the Incarnation," (2) the "mode of union of the Word Incarnate," and (3) "what follows this union" (*ST* III, q. 1, prol.).

"It was fitting that God should become incarnate," because God is the highest good and "it belongs to the essence of the highest good to communicate itself in the highest manner to the creature, and this is brought about chiefly by *His joining created nature to Himself that one Person is made up of these three—the Word, a soul and flesh*, as Augustine says" (*ST* III, q. 1, a. 1; italics in the original).

The fittingness of the Incarnation is a key theme in the *ST*. Because God is omnipotent, it was not absolutely necessary that God become man. God could have saved the human race through means other than the Incarnation. Nonetheless, the end of human salvation was attained in a more fitting, or "convenient," way through the Incarnation (*ST* III, q. 1, a. 2).

The motivation of the Incarnation is a significant element in the "Christology" of the *ST*. Aquinas defers to what God reveals about why the Eternal Word became man: "since everywhere in the sacred scripture the sin of the first man is assigned as the reason of the Incarnation, it is more in accordance with this to say that the work of the Incarnation was ordained by God as a remedy for sin." Hence, "had sin not existed, the Incarnation would not have been" (*ST* III, q. 1, a. 3). Aquinas here continues to illustrate the movement of authentic Catholic theology—faith seeking understanding. Divine revelation, which the theologian receives through faith, provides the starting point of Aquinas's theological reflection. And in light of faith, Aquinas proceeds to reflect upon what divine revelation means.

God has revealed that the Incarnation was "for us men and for our salvation," as we profess in the Creed. Thus, the Incarnation has a very specific purpose that shapes every aspect of this mystery of the faith: redemption. Consequently, the Incarnation is a *Redemptive Incarnation*.

*The Mode of Union of the Incarnate Word (*ST *III, qq. 2–15)*

If *ST* III, q. 1 explains the *why* of the Incarnation—the motivation that accounts for the Second Person of the Trinity, the Eternal Word, becoming man—the focus of *ST* III, qq. 2–15 is upon the *being* of our Savior. What kind of being is Jesus? How is he the kind of being that he is (i.e., a being both God and man)?

Aquinas frames his answers to these questions around three elements: (1) the *union* of two natures—the divine nature and the human nature—in the Incarnate Word (*ST* III, q. 2), (2) the centrality of the *Divine Person* of the Eternal Word in the union of these two natures (*ST* III, q. 3), and (3) the *condition of the human nature* that is assumed by the Divine Person (*ST* III, qq. 4–15).

ST III, q. 2 explains how Jesus is truly God and truly man. The Incarnation refers to the *personal union* of God's divine nature and the created human nature that the Eternal Word assumed. Thus, Jesus is *one Divine Person* with *two natures*: a *divine nature* and a *human nature*. "The union of human nature to the Word of God took place in the person, and not in the nature" (*ST* III, q. 2, a. 2). Following the declaration of the Council of Chalcedon (AD 451), Aquinas maintains that there is a real distinction between the divine nature and the human nature of Christ: "The only-begotten Son of God appeared in two natures, without confusion, without change, without division, without separation" (*ST* III, q. 2, a. 1, s.c.). The critical point throughout this question—and throughout all of the questions dealing with the Incarnation—is that a union of natures (on the level of nature) is impossible. Divine and human natures are essentially different. Therefore, there cannot be any "blending" of these two natures. Nonetheless, there was a real union of the divine and the human natures of Christ. But these natures were not and could not have been united on the level of nature but, rather, they were united on the level of the Person. This "grace of union" signals the gratuitous act of God in which human nature is raised, or "assumed," to the level of divinity, even on the level of existence (*ST* III, q. 2, aa. 10–12).

Nevertheless, this union took place with respect to the Divine Person. This is the focus of *ST* III, q. 3. Because "to assume is to take something to oneself," this assumption of the human nature requires two things: (1) the *principle* of the assumption and (2) the *term* of the assumption. The principle is *that by means of which* this assumption of the human nature took place. The term is *that to which* the human nature was assumed. The Divine Person of the Eternal Son, Aquinas explains, is both the principle and the term of the assumption. The Person of the Son is the *principle* because "it properly belongs to a person to act; and this assuming of flesh took place by the Divine action" (*ST* III, q. 3, a. 1). The Person is also the *term* of the act of assumption because "the union took place in the Person, and not in the nature," as Aquinas has already explained in *ST* III, q. 1, aa. 1–2.

The dynamics of assumption, then, revolve around the Divine Person of the Eternal Son. Aquinas's presentation of the union of natures in the Divine Person of the Eternal Son, thus, culminates in the dogma known as the *hypostatic union* (derived from the Greek word associated with personhood, *hypostatis*). Although the two other Divine Persons—the Father and the Holy Spirit—could have assumed a human nature, it was most fitting that the Eternal Son be the Trinitarian Person to assume a human nature because of what human nature is and what a fallen humanity needs (*ST* III, q. 3, a. 8).

After Aquinas explains the hypostatic nature of the Incarnation, he proceeds to consider "the union on the part of what was assumed." Otherwise expressed, he homes in on the human nature itself that was assumed by the Person of the Eternal Word. "About which we must consider first what things were assumed by the Word of God [*ST* III, qq. 4–6]; second, what [things] were co-assumed, whether perfections or defects [*ST* III, qq. 7–15]" (*ST* III, q. 4, prol.). With regard to the assumed nature, Aquinas considers (1) the assumed human nature itself (*ST* III, q. 4) and (2) the parts of the human nature assumed (*ST* III, qq. 5–6).

Aquinas explains that human nature was "capable of being assumed by a Divine Person" in reference to the *dignity* of human nature as well as according to the *need* of human nature (*ST* III, q. 4, a. 1). Human nature has a dignity because it is a rational nature—it can know and love and, thus, it can know and love the Eternal Word. Because of the state of original sin in which human persons suffer, human nature also "stood in need of restoration." In these two ways, human nature is unique among all created natures (*ST* III, q. 4, a. 1).

In the following articles, Aquinas is emphatic that "the Son of God in nowise assumed a human person," because the person is the term of assumption and not the thing assumed (*ST* III, q. 4, a. 2). Consequently, it is not accurate to say that the Eternal Word assumed "a man." *A man* is a person and not only a nature. "The Son of God is not the man whom He assumed, but the man whose nature He assumed" (*ST* III, q. 4, a. 3).

Human nature comprises parts, and it is to these parts that Aquinas turns his attention in *ST* III, q. 5. He explains that because the Eternal Son assumed a true human nature—a nature possessing all of those good elements that are truly human—the Eternal Son assumed a true *earthly body* and a true *human soul*. Because human nature, by definition, is a rational and a bodily nature, Jesus assumed a human body and human rationality in the Incarnation. Our Lord's humanity is a *true* and *real* humanity. It is not an "imaginary" humanity (*ST* III, q. 5, a. 2). Moreover, there was no temporal succession in Our Lord's assumption of human nature. "The soul and body were mutually united at the same time in order to constitute the human nature of the Word" (*ST* III, q. 6, a. 5).

*The Perfections of Christ (*ST *III, qq. 7–13)*

After examining the nature assumed by the Eternal Son, Aquinas explores those *perfections* and *defects* that were "co-assumed by the

Son of God in human nature." Aquinas identifies three perfections that attended the assumption of human nature: (1) the grace of Christ, (2) the knowledge of Christ, and (3) the power of Christ (*ST* III, q. 7, prol.).

The *grace of union* refers to the "union of the human nature with the Divine Person." This grace of union is first and central for the *habitual grace* that the human soul of Christ possessed (*ST* III, q. 7, a. 13). The reason why Christ's humanity enjoyed habitual grace lies within the very nature of the Incarnation itself. "Christ is the true God in Divine Person and Nature. Yet because together with unity of person there remains distinction of [human and divine] natures . . . the soul of Christ is not essentially Divine. Hence, it behooves [Christ's soul] to be Divine by participation, which is by grace" (*ST* III, q. 7, a. 1).

Because Our Lord's soul had the fullness of grace, the powers of his soul also enjoyed the fullness of virtue. "Grace regards the essence of the soul, so does virtue regard [the soul's] powers." Consequently, "it is necessary that as the powers of the soul flow from its essence, so do the virtues flow from grace." Therefore, because "the grace of Christ was most perfect . . . Christ had all the virtues" (*ST* III, q. 7, a. 2).

Aquinas clarifies, moreover, what he means by "all the virtues." Our Lord had all the virtues that are proper to his human nature. Because Our Lord did not suffer from sin or disorder in any way, he did not have all of the virtues in the same way that human persons have them. Christ had the virtues "most perfectly" and "beyond the common mode" of the virtues (*ST* III, q. 7, a. 2, ad 3). For example, "Christ had no evil desires whatever . . . yet he was not thereby prevented from having temperance, which is the more perfect in man, as he is without evil desires" (*ST* III, q. 7, a. 2, ad 3).

Additionally, Jesus did not have the theological virtues of faith and hope. "From the first moment of conception Christ saw God's essence fully" (*ST* III, q. 7, a. 3). Thus, there was no faith in him. Likewise, "as it is of the nature of faith that one assents to what one sees not, so is it of the nature of hope that one expects what as yet one has not." And like faith, hope did not apply to Our Lord, who "from the beginning of His conception . . . had the Divine fruition fully" (*ST* III, q. 7, a. 4). There was not even the slightest distance between Christ's humanity and divinity. Therefore, Our Lord did not have faith or hope, but he did have charity and the gifts of the Holy Spirit (*ST* III, q. 7, a. 5). In Christ was the fullness of grace (*ST* III, q. 7, a. 10) and all of those gifts that attend such fullness.

In *ST* III, q. 13, Aquinas considers the *power* of Christ's soul. He explains that the soul of Our Lord is not properly omnipotent. The soul of Christ is a part of his assumed human nature. As human, it is created and does not possess the power proper to the divine nature. Therefore, although the person of Christ is omnipotent, the power of omnipotence is proper to the divine nature and not to the human nature. Consequently, all of the supernatural things that Our Lord did were done in virtue of the divine nature. This is why Aquinas says, "He wished things to be brought about by the divine power, as the resurrection of His own body and such like miraculous deeds, which He could not effect by his own power, except as an instrument of the Godhead" (*ST* III, q. 13, a. 4).

*The Defects of Christ's Body and Soul (*ST *III, qq. 14–15)*

After examining the perfections that attended Christ's humanity, Aquinas then considers the defects associated with his humanity. Specifically, he considers the defects of Our Lord's *body* and *soul*. It is important to recognize that the "defects" spoken of here do not fall within the category of moral evil. The defects of which Aquinas speaks are not defective because the humanity of Christ was lacking in some essential way. Rather, the defects that Aquinas identifies are simply those characteristics of human nature that are instrumentally ordered to his work of redemption. This is why Aquinas says that "it was fitting for the Son of God to assume flesh subject to human infirmities, in order to suffer and be tempted in it and to bring succor to us" (*ST* III, q. 14, a. 1, s.c.). Nonetheless, Aquinas is also clear that Jesus did not "contract" these defects (*ST* III, q. 14, a. 3). Christ did not inherit, as it were, the defects of nature because he suffered the effects of original sin. Indeed, "He received human nature without sin, in the purity which it had in the state of innocence. In the same way He might have assumed human nature without defects. Thus it is clear that Christ did not contract these defects as if taking them upon himself as due to sin, but by His own will" (*ST* III, q. 14, a. 3). In other words, Our Lord freely assumed the limitations and susceptibilities of human nature so that he could offer himself and his humanity for us men and for our salvation. Consequently, Our Lord did not suffer any defects or infirmities that were incompatible with the perfection of his knowledge and grace. He only assumed those defects that "are found amongst all men in common, by reason of the sin of our first parent, as death, hunger, thirst, and the like" (*ST* III, q. 14, a. 4). Thus, Aquinas summarizes that Jesus took upon himself our defects "economically, in order to satisfy for our sin, and not that they belong to Him of Himself. Hence it was not necessary for him to assume them all, but only such as sufficed to satisfy for the sin of the whole [of human] nature" (*ST* III, q. 14, a. 4, ad 2).

With regard to the defects of soul, Aquinas adamantly excludes sin from the list of spiritual defects that Christ assumed. "Sin does not belong to human nature, whereof God is the cause; but rather has been sown in it against its nature by the devil." Thus, it was not necessary that Christ co-assume sin when he assumed human nature. Moreover, "Christ assumed our defects that He might satisfy for us, that He might prove the truth of His human nature, and that He might become an example of virtue to us" (*ST* III, q. 15, a. 1). Each of these reasons inveigh against there being any sin in Our Savior. Indeed, "since in Christ the virtues were in their highest degree," any disordered afflictions of the sense appetites were completely foreign to his humanity (*ST* III, q. 15, a. 2).

Jesus did truly experience, however, unpleasant human emotions. "It is written (Psalms 87:4) in the person of Christ; *My soul is filled with evils*—not sins, indeed, but human evils, i.e., *pains*" (*ST* III, q. 15, a. 4; italics in the original). This was a voluntary suffering—freely undergone (*ST* III, q. 15, a. 4, ad 1). Our Lord truly experienced sensible pain. "No one should doubt but that in Christ there was true pain" (*ST* III, q. 15, a. 5). Among the pains that Our Lord suffered, Aquinas specifically lists sorrow and fear (*ST* III, q. 15, aa. 6–7). Aquinas explains that as "sorrow is caused by the apprehension of a present evil, so also is fear caused by the apprehension of a future evil" (*ST* III, q. 15, a. 7).

The Consequences of the Union (ST *III, qq. 16–26)*

The prologue to *ST* III, q. 16 provides an outline of the "consequences of the union" of the divine and human natures in the Divine Person of Our Lord. With regard to Christ himself, Aquinas says that it is certainly true to say that "God is man." Indeed, this statement is something that is "admitted by all Christians" (*ST* III, q. 16, a. 1). Additionally, it is also true to say that "man is God." The reason why it is accurate to say—in reference to Our Lord—both that "God is man" and that "man is God" is as follows: "Granted the reality of both natures, i.e., the Divine and human, and of the union in person and hypostasis, this is true and proper: 'Man is God,' even as this: 'God is man'" (*ST* III, q. 16, a. 2). Of course, Aquinas is not compromising the real distinction between Our Lord's divine and human natures. Rather, he explains that "this word 'man' may stand for any hypostasis of human nature; and thus it may stand for the Person of the Son of God, Whom we say is a hypostasis of human nature." Conversely, "it is manifest that the word 'God' is truly and properly predicated of the Person of the Son of God." Thus, when speaking of the Incarnate Word, it is equally accurate to describe him as both man and God—in reference to the divine and the human nature united in the Divine Person of the Incarnate Word. "In the mystery of the Incarnation the Divine and human natures are not the same; but the hypostasis of the two natures is the same" (*ST* III, q. 16, a. 5). This also explains why it is inaccurate to say that "Christ as man is God" (*ST* III, q. 16, a. 11). There is a real distinction between Christ's divine and human natures, and yet "Christ is one" (*ST* III, q. 17, a. 1). "Although Christ has duality of nature, yet, because He has no duality of suppositum [i.e., Personhood], it cannot be said that Christ is two" (*ST* III, q. 17, a. 1, ad 5). He is truly "one being" (*ST* III, q. 17, a. 2).

The Incarnate Lord had two wills: a divine will and a human one. Because "the will pertains to the perfection of human nature, being one of its natural powers, even as the intellect" is one of its natural powers, "we must say that the Son of God assumed a human will, together with human nature." And because "by the assumption of human nature the Son of God suffered no diminution of what pertains to His Divine Nature, to which it belongs to have a will. . . . it must be said that there are two wills in Christ, i.e., one human, the other Divine" (*ST* III, q. 18, a. 1). It would have been impossible to assume a human nature without a human will—for to have a will is proper to human nature.

"Being and operation belong to the person by reason of the nature; yet in a different manner" (*ST* III, q. 19, a. 1, ad 4). Thus, because there is only one Person in Christ (the Divine Person of the Eternal Son), "so, likewise, in Christ there are necessarily two specifically different operations by reason of His two natures" (*ST* III, q. 19, a. 1, ad 3). "In Christ the human nature has its proper form and power whereby it acts; and so has the Divine. Hence the human nature has its proper operation distinct from the Divine, and conversely" (*ST* III, q. 19, a. 1). In sum, when Jesus ate food, for example, he acted in virtue of his human nature. When Jesus performed a miracle, however, he acted in virtue of his divine nature. Nonetheless, in both instances it was the same Jesus—the same Divine Person—who acted.

We recall, yet again, that the motive of the Incarnation was our redemption. Therefore, it is not surprising that Aquinas emphasizes the *priesthood of Christ* (*ST* III, q. 22). "The office proper to a priest is to be a mediator between God and the people," and thus it is "most fitting" that Christ is a priest (*ST* III, q. 22, a. 1). Christ's priesthood is unique, however; Our Lord is both the priest and the victim (*ST* III, q. 22, a. 2). He is both the one who offers the sacrifice and the very one who is sacrificed. "Christ himself, as man, was not only priest, but also a perfect victim, being at the same time victim for sin, victim for peace-offering, and a holocaust" (*ST* III, q. 22, a. 2). And his self-sacrifice was supremely efficacious. "The priesthood of Christ has full power to expiate sins" (*ST* III, q. 22, a. 3). Christ's priesthood—a priesthood wholly for others, not for himself—is an everlasting priesthood (*ST* III, q. 22, aa. 4–6). Although his Passion and death are never repeated, the power of his sacrifice endures forever. And through Christ's priestly work, human persons are enabled to be adopted sons of God (*ST* III, q. 23). Consequently, adoration is due to the Incarnate Lord, the Mediator of God and human persons (*ST* III, qq. 25–26).

The Things That Jesus Did and Suffered (*ST* III, qq. 27–59)

Aquinas explains in the prologue to *ST* III, q. 27 that "after the foregoing treatise of the union of God and man and the consequences thereof, it remains for us to consider what things the Incarnate Son of God did or suffered in the human nature united to Him." He divides his consideration of Our Lord's earthly deeds and sufferings into four parts: (1) "those things that relate to His coming into the world" (*ST* III, qq. 27–39); (2) "those things that relate to the course of His life in this world" (*ST* III, qq. 40–45); (3) "His departure from this world" (*ST* III, qq. 46–52); and (4) "those things that concern His exaltation after this life" (*ST* III, qq. 53–59).

The thirty-three questions that make up this section of the *Tertia pars* are not intended to provide a comprehensive account of Our Lord's earthly life. It is important to recognize that Aquinas's purpose in this section is not to write a biography of Jesus. Rather, the focus in this section is upon the mysteries of the life of Christ as they are oriented around the purpose of the Incarnation. Therefore, Aquinas consistently frames his analysis of the things that Jesus did and suffered around his work of redemption.

There is no part of Our Lord's earthly life—from his coming into the world to his Resurrection—that is not for the sake of his redemptive purpose. Although other medieval theologians wrote about the life of Christ before and after Aquinas, "he is the first and the only to treat [Christ's life] within a structured unity conceived as an integral part of his speculative Christology."[1] Therefore, there is a fundamental continuity between Aquinas's consideration of the mystery of the Incarnation in *ST* III, qq. 1–26 and his examination of the mysteries of Christ's life in *ST* III, qq. 27–59. The being and identity of the Incarnate Lord are directly related to the things that he did and underwent in his earthly life.

Although this book cannot provide a full overview of all the mysteries of the life of Christ, these questions reward careful reading. This section of the *ST* compellingly unpacks the themes and doctrines expounded in the first part of the *Tertia pars* in the context of Christ's life and work. Moreover, it is precisely in light of a precise understanding of the Incarnation that the mysteries of Christ's life are fully intelligible.

The Incarnation of the Eternal Word was for "us men and for our salvation." This is why Our Lord's name is *Jesus*. "Through Him all men might be saved, therefore He was becomingly named Jesus, i.e., Savior" (*ST* III, q. 37, a. 2). Aquinas's exposition of Our Lord's salvific purpose and work does not end here, however. Through the sacraments, human persons are enabled to meet Jesus, the Savior, and to benefit from his redemptive work. And it is to the sacraments that Aquinas turns in the subsequent questions of the *ST*.

Chapter 14

The Sacraments

(ST III, qq. 60–90)

In *ST* III, q. 60, Aquinas begins his consideration of the sacraments of the Church. The sacraments come at the end of the *ST* not because they are unimportant, but rather because their very nature depends upon—and their efficacy follows directly from—the Incarnation. Jesus Christ instituted the Seven Sacraments (*ST* III, q. 64, a. 2, ad 1), and he is also the key to their intelligibility.

Aquinas explains in the prologue to *ST* III, q. 60, "After considering those things that concern the mystery of the incarnate Word, we must consider the sacraments of the Church which derive their efficacy from the Word incarnate Himself." He then explains that his analysis will proceed from a general consideration of the sacraments (*ST* III, qq. 60–65) to a specific consideration of the sacraments.

Unfortunately, Aquinas died before he could complete this part of the *ST*. Before his untimely death, however, he composed a treatment of four of the sacraments: Baptism (*ST* III, qq. 66–71), Confirmation (*ST* III, q. 72), the Eucharist (*ST* III, qq. 73–83), and Penance (*ST* III, qq. 84–90).

The Sacraments in General (*ST* III, qq. 60–65)

Beginning with the definition of a sacrament, Aquinas writes that "a sacrament is a kind of sign" (*ST* III, q. 60, a. 1). Sacrament always involves something *sensible*. He explains that sensibility is an inherent part of what it means to be a sacrament. Thus, there is no such thing as a purely invisible sacrament. The "sacramental signs consist in sensible things"

(*ST* III, q. 60, a. 4). "Consequently a sacrament properly so called is that which is the sign of some sacred thing pertaining to man; so that properly speaking a sacrament . . . is defined as being the *sign of a holy thing so far as it makes men holy*" (*ST* III, q. 60, a. 2; italics in the original).

The sacraments are also *determinate* in nature, divine institution being at their heart. Human persons do not create the sacraments. It is God who institutes the Seven Sacraments of the Church. "Since, therefore, the sanctification of man is in the power of God Who sanctifies, it is not for man to decide what things should be used for his sanctification, but this should be determined by divine institution" (*ST* III, q. 60, a. 5). Because God is the first and principal cause of our sanctification, and the sacraments are ordered to our sanctification, they depend upon divine institution.

Determinate words are also integral to the sacraments. The words are referred to as the sacramental *form*. The sacramental words are of critical importance because words signify "various mental concepts." Aquinas continues, "And therefore in order to ensure the perfection of sacramental signification it was necessary to determine the signification of sensible things by means of certain words." He invokes baptism as an example of his point: "For water may signify both a cleansing by reason of its humidity, and refreshment by reason of its being cool: but when I say, *I baptize thee*, it is clear that we use water in baptism in order to signify a spiritual cleansing" (*ST* III, q. 60, a. 6; italics in the original). The matter and the form of the sacrament, both, are determinate (*ST* III, q. 60, a. 7).

The consistent emphasis throughout this section of the *Tertia pars* is that sacraments are divinely instituted *instruments* that serve the salvation of the human person. Because the Seven Sacraments serve the salvation of the human person, they exceed the native capacities of the human person. Therefore, God's own divine authority founds the nature and the power of the sacraments, through which God communicates his grace to us.

*The Necessity of the Sacraments (*ST *III, q. 61)*

Why are the sacraments so important in the Christian life? *They are necessary for human salvation*. "It is necessary for salvation that men be united together in the name of the one true religion. Therefore sacraments are necessary for man's salvation" (*ST* III, q. 61, a. 1, s.c.).

The salvific necessity of the sacraments is rooted in the nature and needs of fallen human nature. Human persons are led to spiritual things by means of sensible things. For example, human knowledge (even knowledge of the highest sort) has its ultimate origin in the activity of the five senses. And in the order of salvation, God has instituted a means of salvation proportioned to the human movement from things sensible to things spiritual. The sacraments "fit" human nature (*ST* III, q. 61, a. 1).

Aquinas emphasizes that the sacraments are not magic. They are not impersonal rituals. Rather, it is through them that God himself communicates his grace, healing, and mercy. "God's grace is a sufficient cause of man's salvation. But God gives grace to man in a way which is suitable to him. Hence it is that man needs the sacraments that he may obtain grace" (*ST* III, q. 61, a. 1, ad 2).

It is because of the Passion of Our Lord that the sacraments are able to communicate grace: "Christ's Passion is a sufficient cause of man's salvation." The Passion, of course, has infinite value and merit. Nonetheless, "it does not follow that the sacraments are not also necessary for [the salvific] purpose: because they obtain their effect through the power of Christ's Passion; and Christ's Passion is, so to say, applied to man through the sacraments" (*ST* III, q. 61, a. 1, ad 3). The sacraments extend the saving effects of Our Lord's sacrifice to us, here and now. They place us in real contact with Our Lord and Savior.

*The Principal Effect of the Sacraments: Grace (*ST *III, q. 62)*

Aquinas observes that the sacraments "effect what they signify" (*ST* III, q. 62, a. 1, ad 1). Through the sacraments, "man is incorporated with Christ" (*ST* III, q. 62, a. 1). He explains that the sacraments' principal effect is grace. Indeed, they are truly causes of grace. The sacraments "are instituted by God to be employed for the purpose of conferring grace" (*ST* III, q. 62, a. 1). Precisely expressed, the sacraments are *instrumental causes of grace*. Of course, none but God can cause grace. The reason for God's exclusive ability to cause grace in and of himself is that only he is divine and supernatural by nature. Because grace is a participation in the divine nature, God alone can confer this participation upon creatures.

Nonetheless, God has ordained to employ sacramental instruments in his distribution of grace. God "touches" our souls through the sacraments. "For example, the water of baptism, in respect of its proper power, cleanses the body." But "inasmuch as it is the instrument of the Divine power, [it] cleanses the soul" (*ST* III, q. 62, a. 1, ad 2).

Aquinas homes in on the unique kind of grace conferred through the sacraments. He explains that "sacramental grace confer[s], over and above grace commonly so called . . . a certain Divine assistance in obtaining the end of the sacraments." In this way, "sacramental grace confers something in addition to the grace of the virtues and gifts" (*ST* III, q. 62, a. 1, ad 2). The sacraments give specific graces that produce "special effects which are necessary in a Christian life" (*ST* III, q. 62, a. 2, ad 1).

Although the sacraments are instruments of grace, they do not "contain" grace like a box contains a gift. "Grace is said to be in a sacrament not as in its subject; nor as in a vessel considered as a place, but understood as the instrument of some work to be done" (*ST* III, q. 62, a. 3, ad 1). God is the principal cause of grace. Nonetheless, the sacraments truly are causes of grace in an instrumental manner (*ST* III, q. 62, a. 4). The sacraments really do things in the soul of the human person. Precisely expressed, they do things in the human person because God does things in the soul of the human person through the sacraments.

Aquinas devotes careful attention to the nature of *instrumentality* in his treatment of the sacraments. He explains that there are two types of instruments. The first is called a *separate instrument*, an example of which is a stick. The second kind of instrument is called a *united instrument*, or a "conjoined" instrument. An example is the human hand—an instrument conjoined to the human body.

Aquinas then proceeds to explain how these two kinds of instruments coordinate. "The separate instrument is moved by means of the united instrument, as a stick by the hand" (*ST* III, q. 62, a. 5). The united instrument enjoys causal primacy because of its closer proximity to the agent, that is, the one who is acting. Therefore, in the case of the sacraments, "the principal efficient cause of grace is God Himself," while "Christ's humanity is as a united instrument," and a "sacrament is as a separate instrument" (*ST* III, q. 62, a. 5).

Here we can recognize the relevance of the Christological themes explored in the first part of the *Tertia pars*. The Incarnation was redemptive in purpose, with the Eternal Word assuming a human nature in order to save us. And we see the redemptive extension of the Incarnation in the instrumental causality of the sacraments. Not only did Jesus provide the possibility of salvation for the world on Calvary, but he also continues to apply the power of his Passion to us through his humanity and through the sacraments. "The sacraments of the Church derive their power specifically from Christ's Passion, the [power] of which is in a manner united to us by our receiving the sacraments" (*ST* III, q. 62, a. 5).

*Sacramental Character (*ST *III, q. 63)*

After considering grace (the principal effect of the sacraments), Aquinas turns our attention to another critical effect: *sacramental character*. He explains that "character means nothing else than a kind of sealing." Through the sacraments, "God imprints his character on us" (*ST* III, q. 63, a. 1, s.c.).

In order to recognize the nature of sacramental character—and to appreciate its importance—we must recall the twofold purpose of the sacraments. First, the sacraments are a remedy for sin. Second, they perfect and empower the soul "in things pertaining to the Divine worship according to the rite of the Christian life." Sacramental character is especially linked to this second purpose. "Since, therefore, by the sacraments men are deputed to a spiritual service pertaining to the worship of God, it follows that by their means the faithful receive a certain spiritual character" (*ST* III, q. 63, a. 1).

What precisely does this seal of character do? What is this seal, precisely? "A character is a power" (*ST* III, q. 63, a. 2, s.c.). Aquinas explains, "the sacraments of the New Law produce a character, in so far as by them we are deputed to the worship of God according to the rite of the Christian religion." He then proceeds to unpack what the worship of God requires and entails. "Now the worship of God consists either in receiving Divine gifts, or in bestowing them on others. And for both these purposes some power is needed; for to bestow something on others, active power is necessary; and in order to receive, we need a passive power. Consequently, a character signifies a certain spiritual power ordained unto things pertaining to the Divine worship" (*ST* III, q. 63, a. 2).

This spiritual power—this sacramental character—is instrumental. "For to have a sacramental character belongs to God's ministers: and a minister is a kind of instrument" (*ST* III, q. 63, a. 2). Consequently, sacramental character is the character of Christ himself. "Each of the faithful is deputed to receive, or to bestow on others, things pertaining to the worship of God." And this is the very *purpose* of sacramental character. Those things pertaining to divine worship receive their salvific expression in the "rite of the Christian religion [which] is derived from Christ's Priesthood." Sacramental character, thus, "is specially the character of Christ, to Whose character the faithful are likened by reason of the sacramental characters which are nothing else than certain participations of Christ's Priesthood, flowing from Christ Himself" (*ST* III, q. 63, a. 3). Christian worship is inextricably linked to the priesthood of Christ. And through sacramental character, we share in the very power of Christ's priesthood.

Unlike grace, which can be lost through grave sin, sacramental character is permanent. No sin can efface sacramental character. Because this character configures us to Christ's priesthood, and Christ's priesthood is eternal, the sacramental character that configures us to Christ's priesthood does not suffer effacement. "An instrumental power follows rather the condition of the principal agent: and consequently a character exists in the soul in an indelible manner, not from any perfection of its own, but from the perfection of Christ's Priesthood, from which the character flows like an instrumental power" (*ST* III, q. 63, a. 5, ad 1).

Not all the sacraments confer a character. The things that do confer a character can never be repeated, because, as we have already seen, a character is indelible. All of the sacraments confer grace, but not all imprint a character upon the human soul. One can only be deputed for divine worship once. In this way, Aquinas likens sacramental character to a kind of *consecration*, inasmuch as inanimate things can be consecrated to divine worship (*ST* III, q. 63, a. 6, ad 2). The three sacraments that confer sacramental character are *Baptism*, *Confirmation*, and *Holy Orders*.

*Causes of the Sacraments (*ST *III, q. 64)*

With regard to the causes of the sacraments, Aquinas explains that God alone is able to communicate the interior effect of the sacraments to the whole human soul. The reason for this is that God alone is powerful enough to touch the inner recesses of our interiority. Only God "can enter the soul wherein the sacramental effect takes place" (*ST* III, q. 64, a. 1). No created being, no human person, nor even an angel can directly access the soul. Nonetheless, God can use human agents as instruments to effect an inner transformation within the soul. This is because God remains the principal cause of the sacraments even while employing instrumental causes.

Aquinas is careful to balance God's principal causality and the secondary causality of the sacraments and their ministers. The principal cause and instrumental causes are both truly causes, but they are not causes in the same way. The sacraments and the ministers of the sacraments are subordinated to the causality of God himself. Aquinas precisely explains that the sacraments truly effect changes within the human person as instruments, but only because they are utilized by the powerful love of God himself (*ST* III, q. 64, a. 1).

Unsurprisingly, because God alone is the ultimate cause of the sacraments, it follows that God alone can institute the sacraments (*ST* III, q. 64, a. 2). The sacraments are not the result of human ingenuity, effort, or creativity. Rather, they are an effect of God's wisdom and mercy. God's being, truth, and love serve as the foundation for and the guarantee of sacramental efficacy. Consequently, when sacraments are celebrated by an unworthy minister, their efficacy is not frustrated (*ST* III, q. 64, a. 5). Hence, even if a priest celebrates a sacrament while in a state of grave sin, if he validly confers a sacrament, the sacrament still produces its saving effect. "The ministers of the Church do not by their own power cleanse from sin those who approach the sacraments, nor do they confer grace on them: it is Christ Who does this by His own power while He employs them as instruments" (*ST* III, q. 64, a. 5, ad 1). The sacraments do not confer the holiness of the instrumental minister. They confer the holiness of God himself. And God is always holy. Therefore, he is always able to confer what the sacraments are intended to communicate.

*The Number of the Sacraments (*ST *III, q. 65)*

There are seven sacraments: Baptism, Confirmation, the Eucharist, Penance, Extreme Unction (i.e., Anointing of the Sick), Holy Orders, and Matrimony. Through the Seven Sacraments, God has provided for the spiritual needs of the human person.

Aquinas explains that "spiritual life has a certain conformity with the life of the body." Thus, through Baptism "a man begins to be and to live" spiritually. Confirmation, "in which the Holy [Spirit] is given to strengthen us," corresponds to the bodily "growth whereby a man is brought to perfect size and strength" (*ST* III, q. 65, a. 1). Additionally, as a human person requires physical nourishment in order to live, so the Eucharist provides spiritual nourishment.

Human persons are also subject to various kinds of bodily and spiritual infirmities. Just we require healing and restoration when faced with different kinds of physical ailments, so too do the Sacraments of Penance and Anointing provide for our spiritual needs in these contexts.

Finally, human persons are communal beings. Two of the sacraments are specifically ordered to our spiritual needs in this manner: Holy Orders and Matrimony. "In regard to the whole community, man is perfected in two ways. First, by receiving power to rule the community and to exercise public acts: and corresponding to this in the spiritual life there is the sacrament of order, according to the saying of Hebrews 7:27, that priests offer sacrifices not for themselves only, but also for the people. Secondly in regard to natural propagation. This is accomplished by Matrimony both in the corporal and in the spiritual life: since it is not only a sacrament but also a function of nature" (*ST* III, q. 65, a. 1).

Although all of the sacraments are of critical importance, the Eucharist enjoys an unmatched preeminence. "Absolutely speaking, the sacrament of the Eucharist is the greatest of all the sacraments" (*ST* III, q. 65, a. 3). There are three reasons for the centrality of the Eucharist: (1) The Eucharist is Jesus Christ himself, substantially, "whereas the other sacraments contain a certain instrumental power which is a share of Christ's power." (2) All of the other sacraments are oriented around the Eucharist. (3) All of the other sacraments "terminate in the Eucharist . . . thus those who have been ordained receive Holy Communion, as also those who have been baptized" (*ST* III, q. 65, a. 3).

The Sacraments in Particular (*ST* III, qq. 66–90)

After considering the sacraments in general, Aquinas then begins to examine each of the sacraments in particular. Although there are seven sacraments, Aquinas was, unfortunately, unable to treat each of them in the *ST* as he died before completing it. Hence, he wrote about the Sacraments of Baptism, Confirmation, and the Eucharist; but he only partially completed his treatise on the Sacrament of Penance. Aquinas's disciples attempted to finish the *ST* by drawing from his other writings on the remainder of the topics that he originally intended to cover. The result of these compilation efforts is known as the "*Supplementum*." Although the *Supplementum* is a useful resource, it is not considered to be an authentic part of the *ST* because Aquinas was not directly responsible for its formulation and compilation. We will, thus, look at some of the themes related to the four sacraments that he did write about in the *ST* before he died. We will not, however, examine the *Supplementum*.

*The Sacrament of Baptism (*ST *III, qq. 66–71)*

Because Baptism is the first and foundational sacrament, it is unsurprising that Aquinas begins with this sacrament. Concerning those things that pertain to Baptism itself, Aquinas explains that this sacrament is a *washing*. And this washing has a *visible* or "outward" dimension, which signifies the "inward effect" of the sacrament. This visible element is the application of water to the recipient of the sacrament during his or her baptism (*ST* III, q. 65, a. 1).

Christ instituted this sacrament when he was baptized by John the Baptist in the Jordan River (*ST* III, q. 66, a. 2). The proper matter required by the sacrament is water—and this requirement is by God's own divine institution (*ST* III, q. 66, a. 3). Any water can be used in the sacrament as long as the water is truly and "purely" water (*ST* III, q. 66, a. 4). The proper form of the sacrament is the Trinitarian formula: "I baptize you in the name of the Father, and of the Son, and of the Holy Spirit" (*ST* III, q. 66, a. 5). Through these words, the Triune God (the principal cause of the sacrament) and the minister of the sacrament acting instrumentally (through the words, "I baptize you") are both identified.

Baptism cannot be repeated (*ST* III, q. 66, a. 9). It is a spiritual regeneration or a "rebirth." We can only "be begotten but once" supernaturally—just as we can only be begotten but once in the case of natural birth. Additionally, because Baptism imprints a sacramental character, and sacramental character is indelible, this sacrament does not admit to repetition.

The range of baptismal ministers, in certain circumstances, is unique among all of the sacraments. Although it is proper to the office of the priest to baptize because the priest is the one who consecrates the Eucharist—and Baptism enables one to "approach Our Lord's Table"—anyone can validly baptize in cases of emergency (*ST* III, q. 67, a. 2). Because Baptism is "the most necessary among all the sacraments," God instituted this sacrament such that its matter (water) would be "easily obtainable by all," and that its minister could be any human person—"lest from lack of being baptized, man should suffer [the] loss of his salvation" (*ST* III, q. 67, a. 3). Indeed, in cases of emergency, even an unbaptized person can validly baptize another (*ST* III, q. 67, a. 5).

Because of Baptism's importance for human salvation (*ST* III, q. 68, aa. 1–2), Aquinas explains that this sacrament should not be unreasonably deferred (*ST* III, q. 68, a. 3). In the case of children, baptism should in nowise be delayed. In the case of adults, however, Baptism should ordinarily follow a period of preparation (*ST* III, q. 71, a. 1).

The effects of Baptism are profound and numerous. First, through this sacrament all sins—of any kind—are taken away (*ST* III, q. 69, a. 1). This is why no one can confess sins committed before their baptism (*ST* III, q. 68, a. 6). Moreover, "he who is baptized, is freed from the debt of all punishment due to him for his sins, just as if he himself had borne those pains, [because] his sins are set in order by the pains of Christ's Passion" (*ST* III, q. 69, a. 2). The reason for these profound effects lies in the incorporation of the baptized in Christ and the consequent infusion of grace and virtue (*ST* III, q. 69, aa. 4–5). Baptism has these effects equally in all of its recipients (*ST* III, q. 69, a. 8). It truly opens the "gates of the heavenly kingdom" (*ST* III, q. 69, a. 8).

*The Sacrament of Confirmation (*ST *III, q. 72)*

Being a sacrament, Confirmation confers grace upon its recipients (*ST* III, q. 72, a. 7). Similar only to the sacraments of Baptism and Holy Orders, Confirmation also confers a sacramental character. "Confirmation is the sacrament of the fullness of grace" (*ST* III, q. 72, a. 1). Through Baptism, one receives spiritual life, "which is a spiritual regeneration." In Confirmation, "one arrives at the perfect age, as it were, of the spiritual life" (*ST* III, q. 72, a. 1).

Aquinas reminds us that a sacramental character is a spiritual power "ordained to certain sacred actions" (*ST* III, q. 72, a. 5). The character of Confirmation gives the recipient a power different from that received in Baptism. "For in Baptism he receives power to do those things which pertain to his own salvation . . . whereas in Confirmation he receives power to do those things which pertain to the spiritual combat with the enemies of the Faith." Thus, "to fight against visible foes, viz. against the persecutors of the Faith, by confessing Christ's name, belongs to the confirmed" (*ST* III, q. 72, a. 5, ad 1). A confirmed Christian has "the power of publicly confessing his faith by words, as it were *ex officio* [as a result of their status in the Church]" (*ST* III, q. 72, a. 5, ad 2).

The essential matter of this sacrament is the oil blessed by a bishop—the *sacred chrism*. The proper minister of Confirmation is a bishop. With episcopal approval, however, priests can also confer this sacrament (*ST* III, q. 72, a. 11, ad 1).

*The Eucharist (*ST *III, qq. 73–83)*

The *ST*'s treatise on the Most Holy Eucharist is one of the most famous parts of Aquinas's writings. In these questions, readers are exposed to his full philosophical and theological genius as well as his saintly reverence before this profound mystery. He begins his examination of the Eucharist by placing it in reference to the other sacraments: "Just as for the spiritual life there had to be Baptism, which is spiritual generation; and Confirmation, which is spiritual growth: so there needed to be the sacrament of the Eucharist, which is spiritual food" (*ST* III, q. 73, a. 1). Our Lord instituted this sacrament at the Last Supper "when Christ conversed with His disciples for the last time" before his Passion (*ST* III, q. 73, a. 5). It was at the Last Supper that Jesus instituted the priesthood; consequently, the priest is the proper minister of this sacrament (*ST* III, q. 82).

Bread and wine are the proper matter of this sacrament (*ST* III, q. 74, a. 1). The form of this sacrament is the words pronounced by Our Lord at the Eucharist's institution: *This is my body . . . This is the chalice of my blood* (*ST* III, q. 78, a. 1). Jesus utilized bread and wine in the institution of the Eucharist because by bread and wine "men are commonly fed," and this sacrament is one of "spiritual eating" (*ST* III, q. 74, a. 1).

"It is absolutely necessary to confess according to Catholic faith that the entire Christ is in this sacrament" (*ST* III, q. 76, a. 1). Although "the presence of Christ's true body and blood in this sacrament cannot be detected by sense," faith enables us to know the truth about the Real Presence (*ST* III, q. 75, a. 1). Christ's words, "This is my body," reveal the truth about this sacrament. The substance of bread and wine do not remain after the words of consecration: "*This is my body* . . . would not be true if the substance of bread were to remain" (*ST* III, q. 75, a. 2). The substance of bread and wine are not annihilated in the sacramental consecration, however (*ST* III, q. 75, a. 3). Rather, the substance is "changed into the body of Christ" (*ST* III, q. 75, a. 3, ad 1). This change of substance—this *transubstantiation*—"is entirely supernatural, and [is] effected by God's power alone" (*ST* III, q. 75, a. 4). Transubstantiation is not a gradual process. It is instantaneous (*ST* III, q. 75, a. 7). "The whole substance of bread is changed into the whole substance of Christ's body, and the whole substance of the wine into the whole substance of Christ's blood" (*ST* III, q. 75, a. 4).

Nonetheless, "all the accidents of bread and wine remain after the consecration" (*ST* III, q. 75, a. 5). (We recall that an "accident" is an attribute of a substance that does not belong to the nature of a substance—for example, *blackness* is an accident of the substance of *hair*.) This remarkable fact is accounted for by God's divine power. The divine power is uniquely able "to preserve an accident in existence when the substance is withdrawn"—as is the case in the Eucharist (*ST* III, q. 77, a. 1).

The Eucharist "confers grace spiritually together with the virtue of charity" (*ST* III, q. 79, a. 1, ad 2). These effects follow upon the reality of "what is contained in this sacrament, which is Christ" (*ST* III, q. 79, a. 1). Because the Eucharist "contains" Christ, and because "His Passion [is] represented by it," the Eucharist is the cause of the attainment of eternal life (*ST* III, q. 79, a. 2).

The Eucharist does not forgive mortal sin because a person in the state of mortal sin "is not alive spiritually." Thus, a person in this state is not disposed to the reception of spiritual nourishment (*ST* III, q. 79, a. 3). Nonetheless, the Eucharist does forgive any venial sins one has committed because it is the sacrament of charity (*ST* III, q. 79, a. 4). As such, it also preserves its recipients by uniting them to Christ through grace. This union strengthens them in the spiritual life "as spiritual food and spiritual medicine." Additionally, as "a sign of Christ's Passion, whereby the devils are conquered," the Eucharist "repels all the assaults of demons" (*ST* III, q. 79, a. 6).

*The Sacrament of Penance (*ST *III, qq. 84–90)*

Unlike the Sacraments of Baptism, Confirmation, and the Eucharist, the matter of the Sacrament of Penance can elude easy identification. Aquinas explains, however, "human actions take the place of matter . . . wherefore the matter is not applied by the minister, but by God working inwardly" within the penitent (*ST* III, q. 84, a. 1, ad 2). Sins are, thus, the proper matter of this sacrament (*ST* III, q. 84, a. 2). The penitent supplies the matter of the sacrament, and the priest, as the sacrament's minister, supplies the form of the sacrament: "I absolve you . . ." (*ST* III, q. 84, a. 3). The matter is not consecrated but removed. Sins are forgiven through this sacrament. Aquinas identifies the parts of Penance as *contrition*, *confession*, and *satisfaction* (*ST* III, q. 90, a. 2).

Metaphorically, the Sacrament of Penance is referred to as "a second plank after a shipwreck." Aquinas explains, "For just as the first help of those who cross the sea is to be safeguarded in a whole ship, while the second help when the ship is wrecked, is to cling to a plank, so too the first help in this life's ocean is that man safeguard his integrity, while the second help is, if he loses his integrity through sin, that he regain it by means of Penance" (*ST* III, q. 84, a. 6). Consequently, this sacrament is necessary for any baptized person who has committed mortal sins: "It is necessary for the sinner's salvation that sin be taken away from him; which cannot be done without the sacrament of Penance, wherein the power of Christ's Passion operates through the priest's absolution and the acts of the penitent, who co-operates with grace unto the destruction of his sins" (*ST* III, q. 84, a. 5).

Because Penance does not confer a sacramental character, it can be repeated. God is infinitely merciful. Through this sacrament the baptized receive the Lord's forgiveness. "Penance derives its power from Christ's Passion, as a spiritual medicine, which can be repeated frequently" (*ST* III, q. 84, a. 10). Indeed, Aquinas says that "we must say simply that, in this life, every sin can be blotted out by true Penance" (*ST* III, q. 86, a. 1).

Conclusion

Our journey through the *ST* has come to an end. But the ultimate purpose of the *ST* has certainly not been fully achieved. Indeed, this purpose could never be completely consummated—not from this side of eternity.

We have come to the end of this book, yet many aspects of the *ST*—and many significant aspects!—remain untreated. Unfortunately, but perhaps necessarily, this is one of the inescapable shortcomings of an introductory work. The intricacy, elegance, and profundity of the *ST* have fascinated readers for centuries. Consequently, a single book is incapable of doing the *ST* justice. Proficiency in the thought of Aquinas takes at least a lifetime to achieve, and Thomistic mastery is something that only grace can effect. This introduction to the *ST*—much the like the *ST* itself—is only a first step.

Nonetheless, although the preceding pages are far from adequate before a masterpiece like the *ST*, it is my hope that they have illuminated even in some weak way the splendor of this work. As a literary artifact, a record of thought, an introduction to eternal truths, the *ST* is a stunning phenomenon. Indeed, when Aquinas's biographers make reference to the depth and breadth of his writings, they regard his stunning productivity as something almost miraculous.[1] Only grace at work in the mind and heart of Aquinas can account for his wisdom and output.

Time, concentration, and prayer devoted to the study of the *ST* will progressively reveal a profound truth: Aquinas's thought becomes easier—not more difficult—to understand as one advances. Thomists have pointed out that this fact distinguishes Aquinas's thought from that of some modern thinkers. Entering into the order and wisdom of the *ST* does not result in greater arduousness but in greater clarity and luminosity. Aquinas's wisdom is easier to follow—and even to anticipate—the more that one gets to know his thought.

The major difficulties that the student inescapably encounters in the *ST* come at the beginning of his or her time in the work, not at the end.

The reason for this is clear: the work of contemplation is truly a work, but it is not a work within the objectively arcane. The challenges that all of us, as human persons, face when attempting to understand the truth about God come from our side, not from God's. Consequently, the closer we are to God the more we encounter the luminosity of the one true God and shed the obscurity conjoined to our contingency and brokenness.

A fundamental presupposition of the work of theology and of the *ST* is that God is truly knowable. Admittedly, we will never exhaust the depths of God's infinite being, truth, and goodness. But the inexhaustibility of God does not negate the human quest to know the infinite God. Indeed, it is the foundation for this quest.

God has invited all human persons to know and to love him as God knows and loves himself. This is a divine invitation that proceeds from the largesse of the divine goodness. Aquinas devoted himself to this task. And he composed the *ST* so that we could join him in the ongoing work of contemplation.

It would be the gravest of false conclusions, however, to reach the end of this introduction to Aquinas's masterpiece with the conviction that the work itself is something like an independent end. The *ST* is not an end itself. It points to something—to someone—beyond itself. God is the object and the objective of the *ST*—and of St. Thomas Aquinas.

Here, at the conclusion of this brief introduction, the beginning words of the *ST* are helpful to remember: "The Teacher of Catholic truth ought not only to teach the proficient, but also to instruct beginners" (*ST*, Prologue). The *ST* is a work that is meant to introduce beginning students to the reality of God—in all of his wisdom and goodness. God is the subject of sacred doctrine. Sacred theology is a sanctified impatience. It is the consequence of the human desire to know and love the God who first knows and loves us—not only in eternity, but even now.

A few of the many readers of the *ST* have complained, over the centuries, that Aquinas the person is elusive within its pages. Now that we have arrived at the end of this introduction, it is my hope that this common lament elicits a smile on the lips of my readers. Aquinas would have it no other way. The *ST* was not a work about Aquinas himself. It was a work about someone much better than Aquinas—certainly someone who was much more interesting than Aquinas: God himself. The *ST* is not about Aquinas, because Aquinas is not about Aquinas. Aquinas cedes not because of any personal modesty, but rather because all things cede in terms of interest when compared to the infinite God.

But is this inverted proportion between the creator and his creation not precisely the point? In other words, are we not instinctively drawn to Aquinas and to his masterpiece precisely because neither Aquinas nor the *ST* are about themselves but rather because they are about God? The ultimate orientation of Aquinas and the *ST* toward God is the precise reason why a thirteenth-century religious priest and an unfinished medieval tome remain so fascinating even to the sophisticates of the twenty-first century.

God is inherently interesting. As an infinitely intelligible being, he could be nothing but. And all those who consecrate and are consecrated to this fascinating being share in his intelligibility and interest. Were the *ST* about Aquinas, the *ST* would have justifiably enjoyed far less attention than it has received for almost eight hundred years. Because the *ST* is about God, however, the *ST* is just as relevant today as it was during the days of its initial composition. Why? Because God is always relevant.

The theocentric orientation of the *ST* reveals the deepest and most defining trait of Aquinas's spiritual profile.[2] He was a man consecrated to the truth about God. In this way, thus, we can recognize that those who have murmured against the purported impersonalism of the *ST* have missed the point of both Aquinas and the *ST*. Within the *ST*, attentive readers see not just a glimpse but truly the very heart of the historical person of Aquinas. The *ST* reveals a man who lived only for God. In this respect, through the *ST*, Aquinas shares with us what is most personal to him. And through the *ST* he invites us to find our own most personal joy and delight in the same God.

In the *ST*, thus, St. Thomas Aquinas shows us his very heart because therein he shows us his God.

Notes

Introduction

1. For contemporary presentations of Aquinas's life and legacy, see Romanus Cessario, OP, and Cajetan Cuddy, OP, *Thomas and the Thomists: The Achievement of St. Thomas Aquinas and His Interpreters* (Minneapolis, MN: Fortress Press, 2017); and Jean-Pierre Torrell, OP, *Saint Thomas Aquinas–Volume I: The Person and His Work*, 3rd ed., trans. Matthew K. Minerd and Robert Royal (Washington, DC: Catholic University of America Press, 2023).

2. Leo XIII, *Aeterni Patris*, no. 17. For examples of other papal statements about St. Thomas Aquinas, see Pius XI, *Studiorum Ducem* (*On St. Thomas Aquinas*), and John Paul II, *Fides et Ratio* (*Faith and Reason*), nos. 43–44.

1. The Prologue to the *Summa Theologica*

1. *De ente et essentia*, no. 1. Aquinas is here referring to Aristotle's *De Coelo* I, 5, 271b8–9.

2. For a recent introduction to philosophy, see D. Q. McInerny, *Being Philosophical* (South Bend, IN: St. Augustine's Press, 2024).

3. See John Paul II, *Fides et Ratio*, no. 3.

4. For a description of the duties and activities of masters in theology, see Jean-Pierre Torrell, OP, *Saint Thomas Aquinas—Volume I: The Person and His Work*, 3rd ed., trans. Matthew K. Minerd and Robert Royal (Washington, DC: Catholic University of America Press, 2023), 68–91.

5. For example, see St. Thomas Aquinas, *Commentary on the Gospels of Matthew and John*, 4 vols. (Steubenville, OH: Emmaus Academic, 2013).

6. See Joseph Cardinal Ratzinger, "The Renewal of Moral Theology: Perspectives of Vatican II and *Veritatis Splendor*," trans. Michelle K. Borras, *Communio: International Catholic Review* 32, no. 2 (2005): 357–68.

7. For example, see Thomas Aquinas, *Disputed Questions on Virtue*, trans. Jeffrey Hause and Claudia Eisen Murphy (Indianapolis/Cambridge: Hackett Publishing Company, Inc., 2010).

8. For descriptions of Aquinas's personality and habits, recounted by those who knew him, see Kenelm Foster, OP, ed. and trans., *The Life of Saint Thomas Aquinas: Biographical Documents* (Baltimore, MD: Helicon Press, 1959).

9. Jean-Pierre Torrell, OP, *Aquinas's* Summa*: Background, Structure, and Reception*, trans. Benedict M. Guevin, OSB (Washington, DC: Catholic University of America Press, 2005), 64.

2. The Parts of the *Summa Theologica*

1. See Jean-Pierre Torrell, OP, *Aquinas's* Summa*: Background, Structure, and Reception*, trans. Benedict M. Guevin, OSB (Washington, DC: Catholic University of America Press, 2005), 62.

3. Sacred Doctrine

1. For more about the nature of wisdom, see Matthew K. Minerd, "Wisdom Be Attentive: The Noetic Structure of Sapiential Knowledge," *Nova et Vetera* 18, no. 4 (2020): 1103–1146.

2. Some English editions of the *ST* translate the title of *ST* I, q. 1, a. 7 as "Whether God is the object of this science?" This is not the best translation. The original Latin word is none other than "*subiectum*"—from which the English word "subject" is derived.

11. The Cardinal Virtues

1. This diagram has been adapted from Reginald Garrigou-Lagrange, OP, *De virtutibus theologicis: Commentarius in* Summam theologicam *S. Thomae IaIIae q. 62, 65, 68, et IIaIIae q. 1–46* (Torino: R. Berruti & Co., 1949), 20. For a more extensive consideration of the theological and moral virtues, see Romanus Cessario, OP, *The Virtues, or the Examined Life* (New York: Continuum, 2002).

2. For more on the virtue of prudence, see Fr. Gregory Pine's book *Prudence: Choose Confidently, Live Boldly* (Huntington, IN: Our Sunday Visitor, 2022).

13. Jesus Christ: Our Savior

1. Jean-Pierre Torrell, OP, *Aquinas's* Summa*: Background, Structure, and Reception*, trans. Benedict M. Guevin, OSB (Washington, DC: Catholic University of America Press, 2005), 57.

Conclusion

1. Jean-Pierre Torrell, OP, *Saint Thomas Aquinas–Volume I: The Person and His Work*, 3rd ed., trans. Matthew K. Minerd and Robert Royal (Washington, DC: Catholic University of America Press, 2023), 281.

2. For more on Aquinas's interior life, see Martin Grabmann, *The Interior Life of St. Thomas Aquinas*, trans. Nicholas Ashenbrener, OP (Manchester, NH: Sophia Institute Press, 2024).

Cajetan Cuddy, OP, is a priest of the Dominican Province of St. Joseph; an assistant professor of dogmatic and moral theology at the Dominican House of Studies in Washington, DC; and the general editor of the *Encyclopedia of Catholic Theology* online resource.

Cuddy earned a licentiate in sacred theology degree from the Pontifical Faculty of the Immaculate Conception at the Dominican House of Studies and a doctor of sacred theology degree from the University of Fribourg, Switzerland.

He serves as the general editor of Cluny Media's Thomist Tradition book series and is coauthor of *Thomas and the Thomists: The Achievement of Thomas Aquinas and His Interpreters*. He has written for numerous publications on the philosophy and theology of St. Thomas Aquinas and the Thomist tradition.

Cuddy lives in Washington, DC.